DEDICATION

This book is dedicated in loving memory of my late Grandmother,

Emily Florence (Reese) Kidder

She was one of the many thousands of orphans placed on the orphan trains in New York City and brought to the Midwest to new homes and new lives. She endured more than any human being should ever have to, but she persevered and ultimately lived the American dream.

Orphan Trains & Their Precious Cargo

The Life's Work of Rev. H.D. Clarke

By Clark Kidder
HERITAGE BOOKS, INC.

Published 2001 by

HERITAGE BOOKS, INC.
1540E Pointer Ridge Place
Bowie, Maryland 20716
1-800-398-7709
http://www.heritagebooks.com

ISBN: 0-7884-1755-X

ACKNOWLEDGMENTS

I would like to thank Peggy Sayre for so graciously allowing me to reproduce much of the original text from the Reverend Clarke's books, as well as for allowing me to have the many photos copied from the books. I am forever grateful. In regards to the photos, I extend a hearty "thank you" to my friend Skip Drew for the fantastic job he did creating copy-negatives of the original photos for use in this book. Many thanks to my friend Mary Thompson for graciously agreeing to copy-edit the manuscript. My sincere gratitude as well to my publisher, for believing in my book, and in doing so, helping to preserve a chapter in America's history that should never be forgotten. Thanks as well to Sondra Boliek, Mr. and Mrs. Jack Fry, Lynn Cheeseman, Linda Brennan and Richard Clarke for giving me access to their personal copies of the orphan books passed down to them by Reverend Mr. Clarke.

ABOUT THE AUTHOR

Clark Kidder resides in rural Wisconsin where he and his wife Linda and their two sons, Robby and Nathan, farm 200 acres of land. He is the author of three books on the late screen legend Marilyn Monroe, namely *Marilyn Monroe UnCovers* (Quon Editions, 1994), *Marilyn Monroe-Cover To Cover* (Krause Publications, Inc., 1999) and *Marilyn Monroe Collectibles* (Avon/HarperCollins, 1999). Clark is also his family's genealogist, having traced his *Kidder* roots back to 1320 in Maresfield, Sussex, England.

CONTENTS

"Lord, these are thy little ones in need and thou art the God of the orphan, open the way for these."

- Reverend Herman D. Clarke

INTRODUCTION

An organization called the Children's Aid Society was formed in New York City in 1853 by a theologian turned reformer named Charles Loring Brace. It was to become an early child welfare program for America and was formed because of a pressing need to deal with the many thousands of homeless, abandoned and orphaned children that roamed the streets of New York City. Many of these were the children of the masses of immigrants that flowed into Ellis Island from primarily European countries. Many of the immigrants arrived penniless, hungry, and confused which resulted in children being separated from their parents or relatives in the midst of the mass chaos of the crowds. In its infant stages the Society placed children in homes in the New York City area. In time, the practice branched out to include New York State and some of the surrounding states. The practice became known as "placing out."

As the American West grew there became a severe shortage of workers for the factories and farms that sprang up at a record pace on America's frontier. During the mid and late 1800s, the area we now know as the Midwest was referred to as the West and Northwest, as it was the western-most point to which settlers in any numbers had reached. These were the days long before child labor laws were even heard of and when it was really expected that children, beginning at very young ages, would work right alongside their peers. After all, it was quite often a matter of survival.

The Children's Aid Society would gather up the children from various asylums, orphanages and street corners and promise them a new life on the farms of America's new frontier. While this sounded exciting to some of the children, others were terrified of leaving their siblings or parents, regardless of how deprived their little lives were. Not all of the children sent West were true orphans. Many had either one or both parents who were still living, but unable to provide adequate care for them. As the streets of New York City filled to overflowing with such children, the crime rate began to escalate as the children were forced to grow up seemingly overnight and fend for themselves. Many became thieves, gamblers, and prostitutes and slept on the street. Some became newsboys, delivering papers to earn money for food and clothing, much of which was squandered away nonetheless. It was clear that something had to be done and Mr. Brace was convincing in his arguments on sending the children West to alleviate both the city's crime problems and the country's labor force deficiencies.

The mode of transport for the children was the train. Groups ranging from six to upwards of one hundred children were loaded on the train, along with the Society's agents and were sent on a two or three day trip to a pre-arranged destination. The very first distribution by the Society took place in Dowagiac, Michigan in March of 1854. A notice would be placed in the town newspaper a few weeks ahead of the impending arrival and a local committee would be established to coordinate the placing of the children. Farmers from miles around would attend the distribution, which often took place at an opera house or courthouse. The children would be lined up and inspected, not unlike cattle, and would be chosen (or not) by the various farmers. Often, the children would be asked to perform for the audience and would sing or dance. The lucky ones (relatively speaking) were chosen by a farmer or his wife, or both, and were taken to their new homes in the country. The unlucky children were left standing on the stage or steps, often feeling abandoned once again. Some were painfully separated from their siblings and would shed rivers of tears. In fact, the policy of the Aid Society was to not place siblings together, believing sibling rivalry was a potential problem in the new homes. These rejected children would be loaded on the train and taken to the next stop, and hopefully would be chosen there. Yet others were never chosen and would be returned to New York City. The Society's agents would follow up on the children and make occasional visits to the farms they were placed on. If the new homes were found unsuitable for one reason or another, the children would be removed and placed once again. Some children were placed in as many as eight or more homes before finally finding one that was suitable. A handful were eventually adopted by their new foster parents.

The children would be asked to write the Society at least twice a year and report on their new lives in the country and their hopes for the future. The Author's Grandmother, Emily (Reese) Kidder (orphan train rider) wrote one such letter from Waukon, Iowa the day after Christmas in 1906. She was fourteen years old. It reads (verbatim),

"Dear Sir-

I received your letter quite a while ago but did not answer. I go to school with the children that I live with. I stay at home and help with the work. I have not any photograph to sent. We live 2 1/2 miles south east of Waukon. I do not know of the future years what I am going to do. I think I will be a dressmaker. I believed I will start to sew next summer. Well, I will close this time.

Your Truly,
Emily Reese."

This quaint letter was on file at the Children's Aid Society, which is still active to this day, though it ceased sending children on the trains in about 1929. Between 1854 and 1929, it is estimated that around two hundred thousand children, and even some adults, were sent to new homes on what we now refer to as "orphan trains." It is a chapter in America's history that thus far has not been significantly addressed in history books.

In 1987, a woman named Mary Ellen Johnson formed the Orphan Train Heritage Society of America in Springdale, Arkansas. The society preserves records and publishes the stories of the surviving orphan train riders and holds reunions for the riders in a great many states. They have published a series of books entitled *Orphan Train Riders - Their Own Stories*, which are available for purchase through the society.

In the pages that follow, you will read about the life's work of one of the Children's Aid Society's agents, the Reverend Mr. Herman D. Clarke. Rev. Clarke officially entered in to the employ of the Society in 1900, though he had served on a local committee and helped with placements beginning about 1897. Rev. Clarke was a Seventh Day Baptist in faith and hailed from central New York State. His work with the Society began from Dodge Center, Minnesota, where he lived with his wife and was pastor of the Seventh Day Baptist Church. The Rev. Clarke was a multi-talented man. He wrote poetry, composed lyrics and music to songs, taught school, preached, authored books and was once even nominated for Congress in the first district of Minnesota.

In Rev. Clarke, the Children's Aid Society got all that they could have hoped for in an agent. His devotion to the children and to the Society was incredible. He opened his heart to all those he met and looked for the good in all people. By his own estimate, he placed nearly thirteen hundred children during his lifetime. Most of these were on behalf of the Children's Aid Society, but others were placed through his later work at the Children's Homes he was placed in charge of in Cincinnati, Ohio and Battle Creek, Michigan. He took great pride in his work and would travel thousands of miles by rail each year placing, re-placing, consoling and advising the many orphaned souls that touched his life. The Rev. Clarke received as many as two thousand letters each year from the children, who would often correspond with him into their adulthood, announcing their marriages and the thrill of having children of their own. Rev. Clarke answered each and every one of the heart-felt letters and encouraged the children to send photos of themselves and their new families.

In the course of compiling my family tree in the 1980s, I learned from my Grandmother, Emily (Reese) Kidder, that she was indeed one of the orphans that was brought West on an orphan train. She did not go into great detail regarding her experiences, which I've since learned were quite painful. She told me that she was in an orphanage in Brooklyn, New York from age six to age fourteen. I've recently learned that the name of this institution was *The Home for Destitute Children* and it was located at 217 Sterling Place. Grandmother told me she was brought West on a train by a minister and that she left behind an older brother named Richard who was also in the Home with her. Tears filled her eyes as she explained to me that she was never to see her brother again. Only recently did I discover that it was indeed Rev. Clarke that brought her out and placed her and that some of his journals were in the very town that I live in at the home of Rev. Clarke's grandson's widow.

As his life was coming to an end, Rev. Clarke began compiling elaborate scrapbooks, if you will, for each of his seven grandchildren. These books consisted of typed pages chronicling both his family's genealogy and his work with orphans. Rev. Clarke pasted in hundreds of photos of his family, homes and the orphans. He began work on the books in the late teens and completed them just before his death in 1928. Each volume was leather bound and lovingly presented to each grandchild. The immense amount of work that went into each book is a testimony to the love and devotion that Rev. Clarke had, not only to family, but also to the many people that touched his life, and to humanity in general. I have managed to find six of the seven books, now scattered all over the country. It is from these precious books that I have gleaned all of the information and photos that follow.

Through Rev. Clarke's words, you will be able to imagine how a ride on the orphan train must have felt. The Rev. Clarke walks us through many towns and distributions in several states. You will hear him describe what was eaten on the train, how the children were dressed, who was chosen and who was not. Through letters from the children themselves and observations by Rev. Clarke, you'll read of the triumphs and the tragedies that befell the children as they struggled to belong, and ultimately, how they and their families changed the landscape of the West in their newfound lives. In Reverend Mr. Clarke's own words, you will read about one mans life work and you will come to realize that all of us, whether rich or poor, young or old, can make a real difference in this world by simply opening our hearts to those around us.

Clark Kidder
Milton, Wisconsin
December 13th, 1999

A FEW WORDS ABOUT
HERMAN D. CLARKE

Herman Devillo Clarke was born in Plainfield Township, New York on November 26, 1850, the only child born to Nelson and Maria (Jennings) Clarke. Herman was educated at De Ruyter Institute, Winfield Academy and Alfred University, New York, and studied music at Lyons Musical Academy, Lyons, New York, being a pupil of L. H. Sherwood, father of William H. Sherwood, who was for a time America's most famous pianist.

Herman was strongly inclined to make music his profession and was the author of many songs both sacred and sentimental, but deciding that his duty was to preach the gospel, after spending four summers (1879-1882) in gospel tent work with Rev. L. C. Rogers, he took the pastorate of the 1st and 2nd Seventh Day Baptist Churches at Verona, New York in 1882, being ordained on November 3, 1883. He later held pastorates in Independence, New York, Dodge Center, Minnesota and Garwin, Iowa.

Clarke was married to Miss Anna M. Jennings on September 17, 1874. Anna assisted with the placing of many of the orphan children, even taking individuals in to her home on several occasions. Anna died on May 8, 1912. Three children were born to Herman and Anna: Mabel A. (Mrs. Charles Sayre), Forence O. (Mrs. Arthur Ellis), and Elvan H. Clarke.

While at Dodge Center Clarke became greatly interested in the work of the New York Children's Aid Society and assisted them in placing orphan children in good homes. In 1900 he entered the employ of the society as a full time placing and visiting agent and in this capacity traveled thousands of miles each year looking after the children's interests. In 1911 he was called from this work to Cincinnati, Ohio to assist in building up a Children's Home similar to the New York society. Following this he became superintendent of the Haskell Home for orphan children at Battle Creek, Michigan for about one year.

Clarke was the author of several books and wrote many articles on religious and political subjects. Elder Clarke was a man of strong convictions, deep feeling, and unswerving loyalty to his ideals. He was a loyal friend, a loving husband and a patient, tender father.

Clarke died at age 78 on December 25, 1928 at Memorial Community Hospital in Edgerton, Wisconsin. He was buried in Dodge Center, MN. He had spent his final years at the home of his son Charles in Albion, Wisconsin, spending much of his time corresponding with many of his former wards who looked to him for counsel and encouragement, and in whom he remained interested to the last.

CONDITIONS IN NEW YORK CITY
AMONG THE POOR

The scrupulous care of human life and all virtue in and among the so-called "lower classes" is the product of the religion of Jesus Christ. Fearful was infanticide in olden times and among the heathen. It is said that such men as Plato and Aristotle approved it. Destitute orphans, deformed and sickly foundlings, female children of the poor especially, were doomed to unpitying severity and often death. They were made slaves or sent into prostitution. Witches used their bodies for magic. Later on under some phases of the so-called Christian religion, free children were sold as slaves. Now time and wealth is given in their behalf. It is quite fashionable for wealthy men to endow institutions for the care of these children. Jesus Christ is the head of every social reform. Under Christian influences, unbelievers are willing to give much to humanities welfare. Pliny the Younger established an asylum for fathers too poor to care for their children. About 110 AD the Emperor Trajen founded an asylum for abandoned children. Some five thousand boys and girls were cared for. Contrasted with the present times it is said that there was only one illegitimate child to one hundred fifty in those homes. The fraternity that spread over Europe in the last of the twelfth and thirteenth century, was started by a monk called Guy, for the purpose of sheltering, protecting and educating destitute children. That may properly be called a Children's Aid Society.

New York City probably presents a greater variety of people than any other city. The last I heard there were over sixty nationalities in the public schools. In 1908 there was reported over ninety thousand children there that did not attend school. That for lack of room. That same year three hundred sixty-five million dollars were spent for intoxicating liquors in New York City, while they paid only twenty-four million for education, which included four million for new buildings and additions. One month's liquor bill would pay for one whole year's school bill.

The tenements were such that black harvests of fever and cholery and murder were the only inducements to reform them. Mr. Charles L. Brace, Sr. said in his book of *Dangerous Classes in New York* that the criminal class was mainly from the American born Germans and Irish (1872), but even the children of these classes were bright and promising when given a chance. They seemed to be banded together in "Black Hands," "Black Rabbits," and "Plug-uglies" to murder, steal, and commit any other crime. Many of these, through his efforts (Mr. Brace), have grown to be worthy characters, though that puts no premium on crime. Two thousand Dutch physicians made investigation and reported that from their observation and tests, they found that children inherited the mental and physical qualities of parents, but never the moral qualities. This is a great showing for the benefit of writers on heredity.

Too many of the poor have been led to believe that only the poor have evil things, while the rich have good things and oppress the poor. There are two sides to that equation. It comes largely from the poorer classes being ignorant of the principles of good government, and what law is for. If the law were in the hands of police of their sort, civilization would soon be tenements, vagrancy, want of work, idleness, corrupt legislation, and not least the want of sacred regard for marriage. These are preventable causes. Causes that must yield to a long process of education and proper legislation.

One day, my wife and I visited the various places of interest in New York City, especially connected with our work among the children. At the Babies Mission the morning prayer of our little ones sitting at the table near us was:

"Father, we thank thee for the night,
For the blessings of morning light;
For rest and food and loving care,
And all that makes the world so fair.
Amen."

At noon time in concert the sweet voices repeat:

"We thank thee for this food, and all thy mercies,
Keep us from harm, and make us good children.
Amen."

No prayer was more real to me than *"Now I lay me down to sleep,"* etc., which I often repeated at my mother's knee. The memory of that mother's face, as she looked fondly upon her only boy! These little ones are robbed of such blessings and memories. No mother for each little one to give instruction and inspiration for life, but these homes are doing their best and possibly more than the average home now does, where our worldly mothers and fathers that are all absorbed in pleasure and business and do not really know their children. Here in the city are the multitudes of helpless and homeless ones that we can do no less than try to rescue regardless of color or race or creed. Through no fault of their own they are left to a life of sorrow, sin, and helplessness, unless someone gives them a chance to become useful members of society. The shame and degradation of great swarms of men and women is appalling. We walked through Mulberry Street one day when immense crowds of foreigners, especially Italians and Hebrews, were huddled together, filling sidewalks and roads. Marks of poverty and distress and crime could be seen on their faces. What must be the destiny of those children raised in such environment? Who can measure the capacity for suffering or happiness in them? How early they learn the desperate ways of the older ones. Magistrate Flammer stated that in a single precinct, centered by East 104th Street station, there had been fourteen murders the last eight months. At that time there were ninety thousand Italians in that precinct and the Magistrate said he believed one half were armed. If excited or on a strike, what a menace to the city.

We passed the Tombs. Nowhere in the world is the power of sin more clearly seen than in that prison. A great army of fallen men and women reach that "Wreckage Pool" through home neglect. Black eyes, sunken cheeks, fearful marks of woe! And these are not all from Mulberry slums. Boys of sixteen were there whose unbridled passion for the theater was the cause. A man from a prominent family said that burglary was his crime. Burglary in men of high standing! They were not stealing as some to keep soul and body together with food. There were other reasons. Crimes among women from the social conditions. Many lured by the tinsel and show of city life, by promises of employment unfulfilled, by character ruining wages. Two thousand female "rounders" spend months every year in prison. Not illiterate foreigners. Some, yes, many of culture, who have seen better days. Refined and cultured girls who could be loved by virtuous men and who could adorn any home and make the world better, but destroyed by human monsters. The most of them take to strong drink. Thousands from country homes. Opium fiends, victims of wine, and the card mania. Going a few blocks through the crowd, I asked my wife if she wanted more of it and she said, "Enough!"

Illiteracy was said to cause about thirty-three percent of crime, but there are great crimes among the rich and educated. The want of a trade is a potent cause of crime. A few years ago there were found sixty thousand persons over twenty years of age who could not write their own names in New York City. Sometimes in the city, two to four families live in one room with poultry and even a pig to boot! Every Jew as a rule was obliged to learn a trade and Jews are not frequenters of prisons. Few Jews are even known to be in a County House. I have placed a few Jews in homes, but as a rule they care well for their orphans. Second marriages break so many homes and send adrift the children of the first wife, and they all had to go to an orphanage. I had five wards in Iowa named Randolph. The mother died and they were placed in an orphanage. The father was an electrician in Brooklyn. He married again. I saw him one day in the city and he inquired about his children, though he was not told where they were. He said he had five more children. Two of the five placed had died and the rest are now married, two of the girls having corresponded with me a long time and one still does at this writing. They are grateful to me for my watchful care of them these years.

One of these, placed before I had any care of them, had been whipped and driven about until one evening, almost unclothed, she had taken poison, which did not take effect. She ran down the road to a neighbor's and there I found her trembling and in fear of me, for she had been told that I would take her back to New York. I soon made her feel I was a friend and that she was to be kindly cared for. I placed her, wrote her loving letters and visited her from time to time. She has never ceased to thank me for such friendship and help. She has married happily and has a family of her own.

I have placed many a child whose father or mother wanted to marry again and could not unless they gave their children away first. Said a girl to me whom I placed in a western home, "I have seen many a men go down the fire escape when papa came home." "Sister and I have been locked in our room when mamma had company." Those two girls made me untold trouble in many times placing them. They were at last sent back to New York for discipline and to learn to work at some trade. In twelve homes I placed the elder one, in three years. When being sent back she said she would "get even with me sometime." Two years later, coming from a reform school, she asked my forgiveness and promised all sorts of good things if I'd get her back to the west, which I did, only to later on see her ruined by a theatrical company. At last she wrote that she was married and was all right. Such were a few of the characters dealt with and yet they were wards with talent. One girl who went to the "bow wows" later in life, used to be asked by her pastor to sing selections on certain Sundays and people who didn't attend church to hear a sermon, would go to hear that sweet contralto voice of Miss Alice - .

I believe these could have been saved had the first family taking them held on to them until passing a certain period of danger. People, I am obliged to say, expect more of an orphan child than they do of their own. Their faults seem greater. Are magnified greater. Some people are selfish in taking children. They just want a pet to dress up, show off and doll up. They do not want any responsibility when they take a child, but expect all will be well and harmonious and when a fault is seen they are too ready to have the child replaced or sent back to the Aid Society. The stealing of a cookie or the telling of a lie has caused some to lose their homes. I was sent for to take away a boy of ten years for the awful crime of going in the cellar and sticking his fingers in some jelly. Would they send away their own child for that? A little nine year old German girl was placed on a farm in Nebraska and I was requested to remove her. The reason for removal was "laziness." I found that she was so lazy that she ONLY milked one or two cows, did up the dishes and walked a mile to school. She was but half clothed, lacking underwear promiscuously. The next home I placed her in on recommendation of references, soon requested her removal. No doubt she had faults, but they said that she had stolen some cookies and they would not keep a thief. If many "own children" had stolen cookies and been turned away for it, they would still be on the road.

When a child goes to an industrial school, improvement is seen, and when taken to some good farm home they are new creatures. Their circumstances and environment is so changed that they too are changed for the better. Their morale is better and this is a wonderful change. Regular work is given them and they have the care of cows and horses. Girls have chickens to call their own and there is a natural love of animals, and then there is a discipline and some religious influences, though not usually of the highest type, but enough to have much influence so that hidden tendencies are awakened to goodness. In a short time they are new boys and girls, as compared with the life they were living in the city.

Those who take a child that is homeless and keep him or her until the new conditions have a chance to make a change in them for the better, will have a great reward sometime. It is the rearing of a monument far greater than that made from marble or granite.

I visited a girl in Waverly, Iowa whose foster parents were several times deciding to give up. She was intelligent and good looking and in health, but quite ungovernable at times. Had a disposition to "try saints." A hopeless case they thought. I must remove her. At the last minute they relented and again she stayed. Of course, she would have stayed if she had been their own child, but people don't think of that. That's different they say. But is it? Is not that child's soul just as precious as any of their own if they had one? Is that neighbor boy any better in God's sight than Mary or John homeless? This Waverly girl stayed on and on until eighteen years of age and then began a change. She became a teacher, was loving and appreciative. I received a letter from the foster parents saying they were well paid for all they had endured and done for the girl. She was their comfort and they were proud of her. They had simply held on as though she were their own. Had she been totted about from place to place as some had to be, what might have been the result? Possibly a ruined girl.

I received a letter from a young woman I had placed in Minnesota. She wrote, "I can never forget what you did for me in giving me a good home when I was small and helpless." She was trying to raise her own children now in the principles of Christianity. "Take this boy away and don't impose on any other people. He is only fit for the Reform School," said a man to me as I had to come and remove a boy. "Don't you worry what I'll do for or with him," I replied. I took the little "Arab" away to go to another trial home. I put my arms about him and said, "There's lots of good things about you, my boy. You have done wrong to lie and steal, but you are not going to do that any more. I see nice things you were made for. Some day you are going to own a farm and succeed and I will come and see you. I am going to get you another home and am going to trust you and be proud of you. You will not go back on me will you?" He replied, "No, sir." A year later I visited him and his foster father. "He is an honest boy, as honest as the day is long. I trust him with anything," said the man. What made that boy change for the better? - LOVE. He did not have it in his first home.

A girl in Nebraska was named Helen. She was thirteen years of age when I went after her and she had never known her real name until then. I went to Lincoln after her. Waiting for the time to start, we played and sang together. I had some jokes for her. She had been a constant thief. I said nothing about that at first. We talked pleasantly and became acquainted. Get acquainted with your subject before you begin your preaching to her. Just before reaching her new home I said, "Helen, you know why you were turned from your other home, you know. I am not scolding you. You mean to be a good girl. You will be. I have come to think much of you already. I am going to trust you. I am not going to tell your new home your faults, but I want you to remember that if you do such things again, you injure me, your friend, and my work. People will say to me, "That is the kind of girl you place in homes is it? I don't want any of them." And so you will hurt some other needy girls and hurt me, but you are not going to lie and steal again and this is between you and me. Write to me as often as you can and I will write to you. You are going to be a nice woman." She stayed in that new home for years and I never heard that she repeated her offense. I had many nice letters from her. I do not now know what became of her later on. She has probably forgotten all I said on that occasion, but I can not but believe she is now a good useful woman. Boys and girls are just hungry for love, but so often men and women seem not to make any demonstration of it if they have it. These are but illustrations of so many cases I had.

One fortunate thing in this country that is not in some others, is that there is a boundless hope seen everywhere. The worst are looking for something better or better conditions. Much in Europe seems fixed. There seems no opportunity to rise out of their condition. There is a profound force in American life, a desire for equality everywhere. The illiterate want their children educated. A girl sees other girls well dressed and more refined and she wants to copy them. She may be somewhat sensual, but outside influences such as when she goes to school, hears the Bible read somewhere, hears prayers, and she wants to get rid of her parent-taught filthiness.

Sometimes it is absolutely essential to separate brothers and sisters for their good. It seems awful, but results prove the benefit. People make a mistake when they say they do not want a child that was born out of lawful wedlock. The crime is nonetheless in the parents, but the child is none the worse and I find there is a reason why so many such children are really superior. Children born in lawful wedlock do not always ensure best results. We see that all about us.

For placing we took children from all over the state, from Orphanages, County Houses, private homes and Juvenile Courts. Wherever a child is in need of a home. The sickly and crippled are placed in institutions for such to be healed, educated and made better every way as far as possible.

Charles Loring Brace was the founder of the Aid Society. He started out to reform criminals, but soon found that the best way to reform them was to make a straight tree before it was started crooked. Attend to the twig if the tree is to be right.

When I engaged with the Society it had twenty Industrial Schools, nine lodging houses (in different parts of the city), a home for so-called incorrigible girls called Elizabeth Home (now given up to a boarding school), a Boy's Hotel, a News Boy's Home, an Italian mission, cottages on Coney Island, Bath Beach for the "Fresh Air" children, a home for convalescents who had been to hospitals, and other helpful charities.

All this was carried on at a cost of approximately a million dollars a year, mostly voluntary contributions. The Industrial Schools had about twelve to fifteen thousand youth each year and they were taught the common niceties, and with that, house work and trades. The "Fresh Airs" numbered sometimes twenty to thirty thousand children. By 1900 over thirty thousand children had been placed in private homes, mostly in the west, and many helped find work at wages and many whole families were assisted to take up western homes. Thousands of runaways have been restored to their families.

Occasionally I placed one who had been a news boy. These boys were what we may call unique, none like them in many ways. They were light hearted and ready to make light of their own hard lot. Often they had tattered clothes and looks of exposure. They are as merry as a circus clown and as full of powers to imitate them. Their morals are not the best, but often the soul of honor in defending the rights of others less favored. They borrow of each other, papers and money, and always pay back. They'll decide the last nickel with a suffering neighboring boy. Sleeping in dry goods boxes when bankrupt and eating crusts, they toil on in the strife, tempted to steal and cheat and lie. Some of our great preachers and statesmen have risen from this band of street waif.

The Society has a Lodging House especially for news boys. I attended a banquet given them by a wealthy merchant, who had once been a news boy. He gives this on Washington's Birthday annually. No news girls were invited. The boys filed in between two policemen. They formed a double row and in between the rows they smuggled in a few girls. They went in, but not to the dining hall. The police pretended not to see them. Coming out from the tables or feast, the boys had something in their pockets for the girls. One, handing some

11

to a waiting girl, he said, "Here's something fur yer sick mudder." There were twelve hundred boys in this Home. They had their own orchestra and speeches for prominent men in sympathy with their needs.

(above). News Boys' Lodging House in New York City.

(right). Charles Loring Brace, flanked by sons Charles, Jr. on left and Robert N. on right.

12

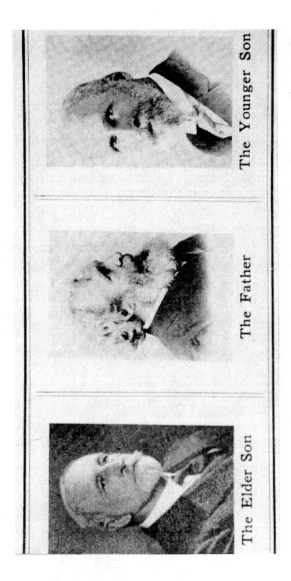

(top and bottom). "Before" and "after" photos of two orphan boys.

METHOD OF PLACING OUT CHILDREN
AS PRACTICED BY THE CHILDREN'S AID SOCIETY

I'll now write of the method adopted of finding homes for the children, as it differs from the average orphanage. The Children's Aid Society came to be called an orphanage, though it was none such, but takes children from others for placing and cares for them in many different ways.

THE TOWN

In selecting a town for a distribution, I found that it was best to go to no city, but to a place of between one to three thousand people, mostly a Protestant town and farming country, where there was good farms and fairly prosperous ones. A mixed population of various nationalities is fair, but when nearly all in the community are foreigners, we do not have much success. I think American and German homes have been among the best for taking children, but there are a few exceptions. Many good Swedes and Danes have been found. I never failed to find at least fairly good homes. Mr. Brace thought Minnesota the best of the states, but I thought Iowa was better on the average.

A COMMITTEE

I then visited all the Protestant clergymen in the town and obtained the names of the principle business men who supported or attended their churches. This was to avoid the impression that the Society was denominational. From these I obtained a committee for reference, etc. of about eight men who were acquainted with the people there-a-bouts. This committee would meet me at the time of the meeting and lecture and in the meantime accept application. In most cases, we would hold our meetings in a hall or opera house, as opposed to going to a certain church, which would make some jealousy or prejudice. Among these eight, at least about four would surely be able to attend. They would be merchants, hardware dealers, physicians, dentists, lawyers and men of different trades and professions. Seldom any women and seldom a minister, for I wanted it to appear that this was no special church or denominational affair. I wanted the busiest men possible, for they are the ones most to be depended on for such work. The men sitting on street corners whittling shingle and discussing the great problems of state and have plenty of time to spare, I do not want. I never failed but once in getting a committee and that was as St. Charles, Minnesota, where only one man, a music dealer, would consent to act. Afterwards, I had the story to tell around that the town was blown away by a cyclone the next year!

A BUILDING

I would then engage the Opera House or a large Hall (not a church) if there was one in the town, for a forenoon and afternoon meeting.

ADVERTISING

I then went to some local printing office and had about a thousand bills (dodgers) struck off for distribution in the place and rural mail boxes, as well as notices in the local papers. These dodgers and notices contained the terms of taking a child, a statement concerning the Aid Society, the names of the local committee and the time and place of this meeting.

The placing of a respectable number of children in a community advertises us and makes people think about taking a child, and so we usually get more applications later on from the same community. In a few cases, we have had two distributions in the same town. Such for illustration was the case at Afton, Iowa.

Homes Wanted
For Children.

A Company of Orphan Children of different ages in charge of

H. D. Clarke, Agt.

will arrive at your town

Thursday, May 4th.

The object of the coming of these children is to find homes in your midst, especially among farmers, where they may enjoy a happy and wholesome family life, where kind care, good example and moral training will fit them for a life of self-support and usefulness. They come under the auspices of the New York Children's Aid Society, by whom they have been tested and found to be well-meaning and willing boys and girls.

The conditions are that these children shall be properly clothed, treated as members of the family, given proper school advantages and remain in the family until they are eighteen years of age. At the expiration of the time specified it is hoped that arrangements can be made whereby they may be able to remain in the family indefinitely. The Society retains the right to remove a child at any time for just cause, and agrees to remove any found unsatisfactory after being notified.

Remember the time and place. All are invited. Come out and hear the address. Applications may be made to any one of the following well known citizens, who have agreed to act as local committee to aid the agent in securing homes.

An example of one of the Dodgers sent out.

17

A HOTEL

I then selected a hotel as headquarters when I arrived. I advertised two weeks as a rule, that being sufficient to aquaint all the surrounding country of the coming of the homeless children. People would be telling about it to everybody and it would be a topic for conversation beyond all expectations. It would be a great novelty, for such a meeting usually was never in that town before. People who had never a thought of taking a child, would want to come from curiosity and interest and many such people took children at the last.

Between that and the time of getting the wards, I would make my annual visits as far as the time permitted.

SELECTING THE CHILDREN

I would return to New York City where usually all the children would have been selected for placing, in number from about a dozen to thirty, babies - up to as old as sixteen, but ages three to fourteen were the rule. The majority of these would be boys, though boys from age two to six were hard to place. The average application would be for a boy or girl from age nine to thirteen, but babies had the preference. When I had a baby or two in the company, the applications were more numerous, for a baby created greatest interest and sympathy. There would be from three to five times as many applications for girls than for boys and we usually had more boys than girls. Very few men in town wanted a boy to raise in the village or city. Sometimes it was necessary for me to go up the state somewhere after some child or several to add to the group. I have occasionally taken other children from Syracuse, Utica, Ogdensburg, Elmira, Binghamton, Albany and Hornell, as well as from County Houses. These children were legally surrendered by whoever has charge of them and some of them were from the Juvenile Court who had rescued them from cruel parents. No children were taken that seemed sickly or were crippled. Occasionally, after placing, a boy or girl would develop sickness or mental deficiency, but on request, we took back any child not wanted.

Method Of Placing Out Children As Practiced By The Children's Aid Society

PROVISIONS

The afternoon before starting I went to some restaurant or bakery usually patronized and made a selection of bread, butter, cakes, coffee, cookies, cheese, raspberry and strawberry jam, cans of condensed milk, etc., which was delivered at the office the next morning in handy paper boxes. For there was to be a two day journey and six meals to have on the trains.

CHILDREN'S BUNDLES

Each child would have a new suit of under and outer clothes, dresses and a few keepsakes. They would come out of a bath and be dressed for the journey.

THE TRIP

This was to be a wonderful thing for children who perhaps had never been out of a city in all their lives. Perhaps there were some of them who were in grief, just parted from a mother not able to keep them, or from playmates they were not to see again. The sights would take their minds off these troubles. We'd leave the office in the United Charities Building on Tuesday noon or there-a-bouts as a rule. We would take a street car, and that was something to call for great care and diligent watching, that all be kept together and no accidents occurred.

The different railways took turns in taking us to Chicago, giving reduced rates; one quarter fare for all under twelve years and one half for older ones, and special rates for myself and nurses. The New York Central, West Shore, Erie and so on. Going across the ferry, we were let on to the boat ahead of all others and arriving at the Jersey side for a train, the conductor let us go aboard first and get seats on one side of the car, two on a seat, seat after seat. This was so we could have good supervision of the children. It was a day and a night enroute to Chicago, arriving in Chicago sometime after noon time the next day. We then took the Parmelee buses for the next station, C. M. & St. Paul or Burlington or North Western (whatever road went through the town selected). On one occasion we had so many children that the Wabash gave us a special car and from Chicago, the C. M. & St. Paul gave us another. There was then another day and night, reaching the next destination on Thursday morning.

Along the way, the children would ask all sorts of questions and would be interested in things they had never heard of. People would give them dimes and nickels and the children would sleep the two nights on the train in their seats and give us much sleepless entertainment keeping them from falling off and on to the floor, or catching cold from exposure. Some would occasionally get seasick. We had a few medicines on hand and things for emergencies.

Reaching the destination, we went direct to the hotel to clean up if there was time, comb hair, tie ribbons on girls, etc., etc. It was a funny thing to have our meals on the train, spreading the jam on bread, drinking and slobbering as children do. The other agents used to serve sandwiches mostly, but I found that it made the children so thirsty that if we did not stand guard over the cold water tank, they would be sick from so much of that kind of water. We used to also take a very large trunk to put their bundles in and then check the trunk back or express it, but later we let the older ones carry the bundles.

All being ready, we marched to the Opera House, usually about 10:30 a.m. Often the streets being full of curious onlookers. As a rule, the Opera House or Hall would be filled. The children were led to the platform in front and seated in a semi-circle. Such of the committee as could leave business were there. A Protestant pastor would offer a prayer and then came about an hours speech from the placing agent, explaining the work of the Society, giving items of interest about the other children placed elsewhere; their successes, the terms on which a child could be placed. Each child was then taken one at a time by the hand and led forward to the front of staging and their name was given, nationality, characteristics, needs (special or otherwise), as well as hints on child raising and some warnings, i. e. "Here is Jimmie, he wants to be on a farm and have a pig or colt. If he can be given one he will be more likely to be contented and happy, not "boy's colt and dad's horse." He is a sensitive little boy, but susceptible to love and kindness." - "Here is Sarah, she is German. Whatever she is, her father is living, but does not provide for her. Her mother died recently. She has an older brother or sister somewhere. She too would like to be on a farm and she likes chickens she says, and if you will give her a few to care for and raise the chicks, and let her have a portion of the egg money, it will make Sarah a very happy and obedient girl." - "This is Petoski. That tells you his nationality quickly. He has no parents living. He was born in this country and will make a bright and useful man." - "Here is a baby, plump and handsome, as you can see. She knows nothing of this big world and will never know her mother. She is in good health and no diseases have been know in the family as far as we can find, to be inherited. The family that takes this baby must have a fairly good home and be able to give her the advantages a child should have. If the home proves as recommended, she can be legally adopted in a year." There will probably be a half dozen applications for this baby. All who apply can not get her of course, but the other families applying will be made note of and if we can later on find another, we will do our best. This in case also of other applications for the same child. " Possibly some of you, not getting your choice, would be willing to try one of the others not perhaps applied for." Sometimes, we had a fine singer, who I would have sing for them. There might be two sisters or brothers or more and we would ask for someone to take them both, but seldom did a family take more than one, and so brothers and sisters had to be separated, but usually at no great distance apart. It was often very affecting, but quite often it was the best thing to do, as often they would quarrel and that would lose them their new home at the start, as often the new foster parent would not stand for much fault in a new child. An orphan's faults are magnified above others.

And so, having made the speech, applications are called for. A sympathetic mother somewhere turns to her husband and says, "We have room for another child, John, lets apply for that brown haired boy," and so he consents. Often a child is placed in a good home in that way, from unexpected parties.

A clerk is chosen by the committee and applications are received. I then announce that at 2 p.m. the children will be placed with such as are approved. "The committee will try to be just to all and if any one thinks a wrong is done, put the blame on me and not these gentleman of the local committee."

All are dismissed for dinner somewhere. My helper, Miss Hill or Comstock, or whoever she is that is helping care for the babies or girls, takes them to the hotel. Often some town families ask to take one or two home with them to dinner and I would reply, "All right, but don't tell them you will give them a home or encourage such, as they might be disappointed and be discontented with some home they do get."

The committee and I look over the names of applicants and then they tell me who in their opinions would give a good home to a child and who is unfit for one (confidentially). Mistakes were sometimes made, which took time to adjust. Often, committeemen would see a child they liked and have first choice. The children are then checked off for placing.

The afternoon meeting draws a crowd to see who gets the children. Especially who has the baby or who gets the red haired girl or the Polish or Swede or German boy or girl. Onlookers are interested in who gets this or that child and are eager to pass an opinion as to the fate of the child there. Some are disappointed. Some wonder why a certain child they applied for is taken by a neighbor. And so it goes. The meeting ends and the papers write it up as one great event of the town. Names of families who get children are given. It is then my duty during the next two or three days to visit all the homes where children are taken and see for myself if all is O.K. or fairly well. The contract is signed and the child left for the next annual visit or until the family may possibly ask for removal during the year. It is a great dread I have to be obliged to tell some family that a mistake is made and that I can't let the child stay with them. It may have been an unusually bright girl that was sent to a very untidy home. The committee does not know all the family lives and homes, only as they may be reputed good citizens and pay their just debts, but the disposition and neatness or foulness of the home is unknown to them.

Method Of Placing Out Children As Practiced By The Children's Aid Society

Probably a large percentage of the children have to be replaced in a year or three, sometimes in a very few months. They think or I think the child does not fit in the family. They may rob the older one of school or something happens or they aren't happy and a replacing must be made. Sometimes a child is not applied for and has to be taken back or boarded somewhere until I find a home elsewhere or put the child into the next company for distribution. A very small percent of foster parents ask for adoption. Some wait several years to see if it is going to be permanent.

Statistics show that eighty-seven percent turn out well, as the world views it. About six percent had to be returned to New York for various reasons. About three girls out of a hundred turned out rather bad, usually from environment or physical inheritance. On my list of over a thousand wards I looked after, I can not remember more than a dozen deaths in the fifteen years I did such work. Three of my boys were sent to the Reform School and about a half dozen girls. One of these boys had stolen a few dollars, which the man had owed him and did not wait for us to settle his rights. In this case I took him out of the home and sent him back to New York. Another had set fire to some buildings where he had been mistreated and was sent to Eldora, Iowa before I could reach him to take him in charge. He wanted to stay at the Reform School, for he said he was better treated and clothed and fed there, than where he had lived. He came out with honor and enlisted and served his country in the Great War of 1914-1918.

It is said that when the placing out of children was proposed, many objections were offered. The people of the country would not want such children or would want them for the help (cheap) they could get it. The farming classes would overwork them and make slaves of them. Some prudish women of fashion declared that farmers and their wives were illiterates and so uncouth that their homes were not fit for them. Even some lady agents had false notions. Then, too, these children would corrupt the morals of the virtuous where they were placed and they would spread contagion all over. Horrible accidents would happen on the journey. How could homes be found? Who could do such work? How could the rights of children be safeguarded? Should they be adopted or given away at random?

I had heard of some Roman Catholic Societies placing them among Catholics quite at random IF they were only Catholics.

State laws are rather strict in some states about placing wards. I found that Catholics of all others had a "pull" on some state officials in this manner, controlling or influencing Boards of Control and had been careless in their work. I had evidences of that Catholic influence in one state and some correspondence with the State Board of Control that did not permit me to have the same opportunities given Catholics.

I placed quite a number of children among Seventh Day Sabbath keepers, where they grew up, united with the church and became useful members. The vast majority of course went to Sunday keepers and many united with their churches, and a great many, especially boys, never united with any church. It is a great thing to grow up what is considered a "good citizen," but it is far better to become a good Christian. Good citizens are not saved. One criticism I made of certain professed Christian families was that they seemed to have less interest in the religious education and salvation of an orphan than of others in the family or neighborhood. This was even evidenced among Sabbath keeping Christians.

There were freaks among those who made application for children. Beauty seemed to be the first consideration or qualification for placing, especially among men. Very many people seemed desirous to have a pretty girl to "show off." Not having enough children to satisfy all the applicants at New Sharon, Iowa, I received something like this: "Mr. Clarke, I want a little girl with curly black hair and black eyes, pleasant features, good form, a good singer and a good memory, so as to take part in Sunday School concerts, and a complexion that will not tan or freckle in the sun." I never found the child! Later on, this applicant had one of her own, a sickly child, and I secured a girl for her large enough to help her in the house. On another occasion, I had an application from a minister's wife. She said they owned two houses of their own besides living in the church parsonage. They had four children of their own who wanted to share their blessings with two homeless waifs. When I went to New York City after a company of children, she wrote that she wanted me to get them a boy and girl from about four to eight years of age, and that I was to take them to

Fowler and Wells, the Phrenologists, and have their heads examined. If all right, I was to bring them, but they must be born between December 23rd and July 23rd, as she got along with that kind of people best. I failed to get the children. Evidently she had been studying the Almanac or Astrology. Most applicants, however, were reasonable as to age and complexion and makeup of the child.

The *Cedar Rapids Republican*, in the editor's pitiable ignorance, heartlessly scorned me for placing children in Iowa. He claimed they were ALL criminals and with criminal instincts, etc., but the state and town press as a rule, gave me most cordial help and sympathetic attention.

DISTRIBUTIONS

William S. Dutton, in the January 1928 edition of *American Magazine*, tells how proud he was of being an orphan and that through that "blessing" he was enabled to get such a good start in life. He was nearly grown, he says, before he learned that he was something to be felt sorry for. The discovery came as a shock and "made him mad." He was so glad he was not "farmed out to relatives."

While there are great advantages in having parents, there are advantages in being an orphan. Although, in my experience, there are two sides to the question. Many orphans I have placed in homes were a thousand times better off than they would have been to have been left even with parents, such as they had. Nevertheless, there can nothing take the place of good parents, parents with means to give the children a decent education, and greater yet, bring them up in the fear of God.

What I would like to write would fill volumes. This chapter may seem long, but it is but an outline of all the experiences and education I myself got out of it, and what eighty-seven percent of the children got out of it. It shows that while heredity is a great thing and all have hereditary traits of character, environment does the greatest part for us in life. The Race Betterment Conference to the contrary notwithstanding.

My engagement with the New York Children's Aid Society came gradually, as follows: Mr. E. Trott, Placing Agent of this Society, came to Dodge Center, Minnesota to arrange for the placing of a company of children on May 24th, 1898. Upon organizing a committee for reference, etcetera. I was asked to be one of that Committee.

My first experience in placing needy children in homes was in the spring of 1897. There came to me from Marion, Kansas, a father with three children, a girl and two boys. He asked me to find him work and his children homes. The mother had recently died. They were Seventh Day Baptists. The father of the children was named H. P. Grace and was in middle life. These were as forlorn a looking lot as I had ever seen. The poor girl had been sadly neglected. Her name was Lillie. My wife fixed her up and soon had her presentable. The boys were Wardner and Mortimer. I found work for the father and soon had the girl well located in the good family of Ernest Glawe, Germans, and members of the Seventh Day Baptist Church. Wardner was also provided for temporarily. I do not know where he finally went, but he grew to manhood and I heard he was from a mere worldly point of view, successful. I took Mortimer "Mortie" to Chicago on April 25th, 1897 and he was put in the care of Reverend D. B. Coon. He then went to the family of Deacon Whitford of Farina, Illinois. The boys have grown to manhood, but I never have had a word from them in any way of appreciation for what was done for them. Lillie was a very nice girl, was baptized and united with the Dodge Center Seventh Day Baptist Church. She very soon learned to speak German well, as well as English. The father married after that, but never has written me a word since I placed his children. Lillie grew to beautiful womanhood and at last married in Minneapolis in 1915.

I always made each boy and girl and each trip a subject of special prayer:

"Lord, these are thy little ones in need and thou art the God of the orphan, open the way for these."

DODGE CENTER, MINNESOTA - MAY 26th, 1898

Children placed were:
John Burch
Mary Dugan
Charles Halpin
William Hunecke
William Malony
Patrick O'Brian

Anthony Remer
August Schuck
John Schuck
Fred Stenger
William Jennings VanSlyke
Harry Wright

Placed later were:
Kathleen Marie Belt
Reva Brewster (see also Manilla, Iowa distribution)
Reginald Collier
Carmine Denairo (placed with Mr. and Mrs. A. N. Langworthy)
Jessie Denairo (placed in same home as sister, above)
Amanda Fahr (placed with A. Scovel at Elkport, Iowa and then with
  Urias Kerr of Wadena, Iowa-then came to Dodge Center)
Ida May Fahr (placed in same homes as sister above)
Louis Jones (placed with Arthur E. Ellis)
George Lachnauer
Florence McGuire (see also Winnebago, Minnesota distribution)
Henry Schaupye
Ina Lillian Stevens
Charles Vetter
Jennie May White

      The company came on the date above indicated. The meeting was held in Thuet's Hall and the children placed. Being my home town I mention for history the following names, those who came first with Mr. E. Trott and others I placed later on there. Mr. Trott was a fine gentleman, somewhat aged. He had previously been to see me and others, asking that we be a reference committee to assist him in the placing or distribution. This Committee was to look over the applications that might be made after he gave his talk in the Hall, and we were to decide who in our opinion were the best families in which to place the children. This we did on the date mentioned, and all were seemingly well pleased.

The most interesting of these was a little Italian girl named Carmine Denairo. She was the first girl I placed in a home from the New York Children's Aid Society. She was previously in the New York Infant Asylum. She was born about November 13th, 1890, though we never knew exactly the age of she and her sister Jessie. Carmine was taken into the Seventh Day Baptist home of Mrs. S. of Dodge Center, but the foster mother had an impression that all Italians were musicians by inheritance and she could not give her the musical education required. At least that was the excuse she gave for giving up Carmine to be replaced after about three months. I took her to my home for a few weeks until I found a suitable home. One day in a joke I said to a dear friend, "You need this girl. She will be a means of grace to you." I was mostly joking. He had no children of his own. He replied, "No, I do not like children." In a few days he came and said he would give my wife a rest and take the child to his home for a visit. That was in November of that year. She never returned. Her new foster parents were Mr. and Mrs. A. N. Langworthy who lived near town. She became a household necessity and comfort and the family did grandly by her. Carmine grew up there a specialist in judging and raising fancy poultry, and in domestic affairs. No musical ability was ever seen to develop, but she was a good girl. She united with the church at Dodge Center and later on, when her sister Jessie married and went to Battle Creek, she too went, married a soldier named Willis Poulter from Camp Custer and then suddenly died of the "flu."

Jessie Denairo was born about January 27, 1889. She was placed first at Rockford, Iowa in 1895, then at Nora Springs, Iowa October 25th, 1895 and yet again at Center Point, Iowa in 1899. At this point I might mention that when I went to Iowa to live, word came to me to remove Jessie, who was at Center Point, Iowa. Carmine had not seen or heard from her in four years and knew not where she was. It was October 1899. Jessie was placed at least three times. The family having Jessie quarreled over the girl, the man wanting to keep her, the woman and son not wanting her. The wife and son had taken the matter to a lawyer. I got her and took her to my home at Garwin, Iowa. My wife took her to Carmine's home (A. N. Langworthy's) on November 3rd of that year, where she grew up. She had music in her and became a pianist. She had elocutionary abilities and took first prize over all the High Schools in the county in a contest. She studied elocution and later in life was able to do much good in public and with other young people. She taught school. She married a man from Grand Marsh, Wisconsin in 1914 named John Carter. They then went to Battle Creek, Michigan and have a home and four children at this writing (1928). She is active in church affairs, especially Sabbath School, training others in her art.

Amanda Fahr was born February 22nd, 1884. She was first placed at A. Scovel's at Elkport, Iowa and then with Urias Kerr of Wadena, Iowa. She married on April 20th, 1910 to Carlton Brown and moved to Battle Creek, Michigan. They have two daughters.

Ida Fahr was born about May 1st, 1889. She was placed in the same two homes as her sister above, prior to being placed in Dodge Center. She too went to Battle Creek, Michigan and later graduated as a nurse. She and Amanda have brothers Harry and William Fahr.

Louis Jones was born December 3rd, 1891. He was replaced on July 26th, 1901 and then again in Dodge Center April 28th, 1904. He was of Welsh descent. He later went to Lincoln, Nebraska.

Florence McGuire was born May 18th, 1895 in New York City. She was placed from the Winnebago, Minnesota company on January 11th, 1907 and replaced on April 5, 1909 with Mrs. H. E. Cook of Wasioja, Minnesota. She married a soldier named George E. Yates. I visited them October 14th, 1925.

Two of what seemed the most undesirable boys, turned out to be among the most industrious and saving when at last they were old enough to get wages. They were John and August Schuck, ages thirteen and twelve, respectively. One was returned to New York City, but he came back pleased with the Northwest. Several never seemed to have any appreciation for what had been done for them. As a rule, girls manifest the most appreciation and are more demonstrative than boys.

Ina Lillian Stevens was born January 10th, 1892. Her parents were Frank and Edna. She was replaced in Plainview, Minnesota on December 5th, 1902 and was placed again on September 16th, 1905 and again on December 2nd, 1907, and again on February 24th, 1908. She married a Mr. Warner in Owatonna, Minnesota.

Charles Vetter was born January 14th, 1895. He has a brother named Joe Vetter. Their parents separated. They came west with the Cumberland, Iowa company of May 16th, 1903. Charles went to Atlantic, Iowa and later to Griswold, Iowa. He went to Manilla, Iowa on April 15th, 1904. On July 13th, 1904 he was placed in Mapleton, Iowa and finally on February 23rd, 1905 he was placed with Frank Brown of Dodge Center, Minnesota. His brother Joe visited him on October 28th, 1905. Soon after Charles ran away, presumably to find his brother Joe.

Mr. Trott asked me to have an oversight of these children he placed at this time and assist to replacing if any needed it later on. This was the introduction to this work , though I continued my pastorate.

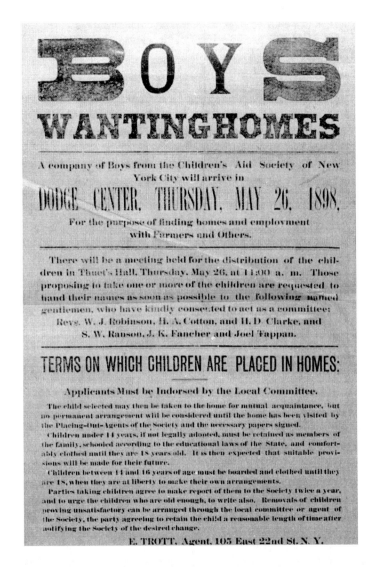

BOYS
WANTING HOMES

A company of Boys from the Children's Aid Society of New York City will arrive in

DODGE CENTER, THURSDAY, MAY 26, 1898,

For the purpose of finding homes and employment with Farmers and Others.

There will be a meeting held for the distribution of the children in Thuet's Hall, Thursday, May 26, at 11:00 a. m. Those proposing to take one or more of the children are requested to hand their names as soon as possible to the following named gentlemen, who have kindly consented to act as a committee:

Revs. W. J. Robinson, H. A. Cotton, and H. D. Clarke, and
S. W. Ranson, J. K. Fancher and Joel Tappan.

TERMS ON WHICH CHILDREN ARE PLACED IN HOMES:

Applicants Must be Indorsed by the Local Committee.

The child selected may then be taken to the home for mutual acquaintance, but no permanent arrangement will be considered until the home has been visited by the Placing-Out-Agents of the Society and the necessary papers signed.

Children under 14 years, if not legally adopted, must be retained as members of the family, schooled according to the educational laws of the State, and comfortably clothed until they are 18 years old. It is then expected that suitable provisions will be made for their future.

Children between 14 and 16 years of age must be boarded and clothed until they are 18, when they are at liberty to make their own arrangements.

Parties taking children agree to make report of them to the Society twice a year, and to urge the children who are old enough, to write also. Removals of children proving unsatisfactory can be arranged through the local committee or agent of the Society, the party agreeing to retain the child a reasonable length of time after notifying the Society of the desired change.

E. TROTT, Agent, 105 East 22nd St. N. Y.

The Dodger used to announce the arrival of the Dodge Center, Minnesota company of May 26, 1898.

Carmine (back center) and Jesse Denairo (back right), seated with Mr. and Mrs. Langworthy, their foster parents. Photo was taken November 14, 1910 on an Anniversary of the Langworthy's.

Amanda (l) and Ida Fahr (r).

LIME SPRINGS, IOWA - SEPT. 7-8th, 1898

Children placed were:
William Atha
Max Bareter
Amelia Engler
John Gould
Augusta Heilman (placed four years later at Spring Valley, MN)
Emma Heilman (placed four years later at Spring Valley, MN)
Ernest Heilman
August Kaherbeck
A German boy

In September I arranged for a distribution for Mr. Trott at Lime Springs, Iowa. We had there for a leading Committeeman, a Mr. H. G. Kaiser, who took a girl named Amelia Engler, who later on was replaced with a Mr. Newell in Walker, Iowa. She was a brilliant, scholarly girl and when I visited her she recited her graduating oration to me, which was exceptionally fine. She wrote short stories and sketches beyond her years. She married a man in her locality. Mr. Kaiser had taken another girl who was also ambitious and she graduated from Lenox College in 1907 and taught school in 1908.

In some respects this was a successful placing and several were destined to become prominent in life. A few others had a rather tragic life.

William Atha was replaced and fell into bad hands. They worked him fearfully seven days in the week and half clothed him. I went after him, compelled them to buy him good new clothes and then brought him home with me and placed him at wages near Dodge Center. I would have sued for his wages, had there been a lawyer in town, but it was probably well I did not. One evening, at the end of the season, he came to me well dressed, saying he was going up into the lumber camps in Northern Wisconsin. I begged him not to, as he would learn profanity, drinking and other bad habits, for there is no refining influence of women there and they are a profane set that smoke and drink. "Go hike off into Iowa somewhere and attend High

School in the winter, working for your board," I said to him. He did so, graduated at High School and went to the Pella Baptist College and wrote me saying he was going to study for the ministry. He graduated, as I received his graduation card, but I guess he did not enter the ministry. Once or twice he wrote me, but then stopped. Though I had "put him on his feet" and been his salvation, he never thanked me or showed me any attention in reply to my interest in him. It is satisfying though to know that he did not go to the logging camps and he received a fine education.

Max Bareter was born January 7th, 1890. He died suddenly in the winter of 1907/8.

One of these Lime Springs boys, John Gould, had a very checkered career. The Superintendent of the Poor brought him to me at Garwin, Iowa from the north and he was seemingly partially insane. I had at one time had to hold him by main force in my home to keep him from running back to Lime Springs. After he had cooled off and acknowledged himself ashamed, I hired him out for wages and he was just crazy after money. One man for whom he worked refused to pay his wages, as he had broken a pitchfork. I told the man that I did not care if he had broken a dozen pitchforks, he'd pay that boy his wages or I'd sue him. He paid. Later on John became utterly unmanageable, but again tamed down. After I had moved away, the people raised him money and he was sent to New York City, assisted by Garwin friends. He went with a cattle man to Chicago and lost or spent all his money, to the disgust of his benefactors, and he came right back to them. After a tragic career he disappeared. Of course, such a boy will prejudice many against boys from New York who are to be placed.

Two brothers in the company were destined to be leading in some industry. The Heilman boys. One became an electrician and had charge of the electric light plant. Later at Spring Valley, Minnesota, I placed two of their sisters, who now are married and have fine men and good homes. Emma Heilman, the older sister, was born August 4th, 1888. She was replaced later from the Spring Valley, Minnesota company on July 26th, 1901. She "did not fit in the family" they said. Nor in her second home. I took her home with me for a month and placed her again, and then again. She was a most beautiful girl, but somehow families seemed not to like her. At last I placed her at Rochester, Minnesota with J. M. Jacks, put restrictions on her, and from that time she went ahead in her education. Emma Heilman graduated from High School, taught successfully a few years and married Cris Hare, one of the famous Mayo brother's clinic men at Rochester, Minnesota on October 27th, 1915. They have two children. When I was seriously sick for seven months at Dodge Center, Minnesota she came to see me, bringing a pretty flowering plant. That was the spring of 1923.

Augusta Heilman was born January 30th, 1890. Augusta Heilman was legally adopted by a German. She grew up and married an industrious farmer named Henry Besingfas on October 11th, 1911. They own two good farms and have a family of two fine girls, whose pictures I took on a visit on October 4-5th, 1925. Emma and Augusta have two brothers named Ernest and William.

August Kaherbeck was born August 11th, 1890. He was again placed in 1901 in Spring Valley, Minnesota. He caused me some trouble and on March 1st, 1908 was sent back to New York City, and yet he had good qualities.

Another German boy in this company, who had roamed from home to home, at last inherited several thousand dollars from someone in Germany. He put his papers in a bank in Iowa and wrote to me to help him invest his money. He wanted to invest in a chicken ranch at Minneapolis and said he could get the land for about twelve dollars an acre. Poor boy, he knew little of values. According to his former foster mother, he had his hand injured and when a doctor who was to operate on it used a handkerchief soaked with chloroform, he died under the anesthetic. I could not find where his money went and he was buried by the Poor Master. Thus, the introduction to this work made more sure, I began what was to be my life's work.

(top). Max Bareter.

(bottom). Amelia Engler.

WILLIAMSBURG, IOWA - OCTOBER, 1899

Children placed were:
Thomas Demourjin
A Boy
A Boy
A Boy
A Girl

In October of 1899 I went to West Union, Iowa and two other towns after some children to be replaced. One girl and the rest boys. The girl I sent to a friend of mine at Gladbrook, Iowa. The boys were taken on to Williamsburg. Mr. Trott and myself had a distribution at Williamsburg, Iowa and among the children was a little Armenian boy, Thomas Demourjin. He was born July 26th, 1890. His father had been shot by the Turks. His mother and a sister escaped to this country, aided by missionaries. The mother and sister remained in New York City and later visited Thomas on their way to California. He was taken by an unmarried brother and sister on a farm. He was made fun of by American children, but soon outstripped them all in school and took first prize in an oratory entitled "My Native Land" and second in carpentry. On June 8th, 1911 he graduated with high honor from the High School. His work on the farm gave him muscle and the quietness and homelike atmosphere of farm life was his making. He went to California State University in Berkley, studied law and set up practice among a colony of Armenians in Fresno. His correspondence has been very interesting. I had in print his oration about his native people, etc. I had many fine letters from him and one dated December 23rd, 1914, I make the following excerpts from:
"Dear Mr. Clarke,

Your highly interesting letter reached me some time ago. Your sketch is certainly to be appreciated by your posterity. I am of the opinion that more family pride than is present in the average American home would be beneficial to the strength of the nation because of the strengthened fundamental unit, keeping it purer. Family pride based on achievement, is nothing to be despised. My present plan is to study law for three years. The service you speak of I am planning to give to my people in this state. In Fresno County is a considerable Armenian settlement who have need of a community leader and friendly advisor. I have never been enthusiastic about returning to Armenia or Turkey. I am not an enthusiastic worshipper of sects and nationalities who wish to jeopardize the good of hundreds of thousands of individuals for the sake of establishing national entity. The outlook for a new era in Turkey must be very different from any we have seen the last twenty-five years to justify such a hope in the most hopeful. The present crisis should have a favorable ending for the Armenian. Without Germany to back her, Turkey is quite likely to leave the map. Russian rule however bureaucratic, means opportunity to Armenians, but there will have to be great sifting and classifying by the migration of radically different types and races, such as we have never heard of before, if even good government is established. May you be blest by many more years of health and active mental life in which to survey the fruitage of your work." Thomas Demourjin Wallace   (He took the name of his foster parents-Wallace).

In December I had five boys at North English, Iowa to replace. In this beginning of my real orphan work, I had more applications for children than I could supply. I continued so much as my church would permit until I resigned the Garwin, Iowa pastorate and moved back to Dodge Center, Minnesota about the middle of September 1900. After purchasing a home at Dodge Center and getting settled, I began devoting more time to the work.

As there will be much to record later on, I will pass over a year or two until I am fully settled in to the work. At first, I was paid three dollars a day plus expenses for special trips. Later, I was paid by the month.

In January of 1901, I made an Iowa trip of seventeen days, visiting sixteen towns, traveling seven hundred thirty-one miles by rail, changed cars twenty-seven times, drove seventy-seven miles with livery. I made the usual reports to the Society.

In July 1901 I went to Sheridan, Missouri to replace two boys (brothers). I knew nothing of the boys nor the circumstances of their home, and knew nothing of where I was to place them. I found them nice little fellows and with their foster father. The foster mother I think had deserted them. They were Henry and Francis B., aged nine and five years. Securing a carriage, the foster father went with me towards Grant, Missouri and we heard of a Mr. Marshall that might take boys. We reached there about dinner time and mentioned our object and were told that they hardly cared to take the boys, but invited us in to dinner and we stayed. During the dinner hour the family eyed the two homeless and motherless boys closely and pity and love began to be manifested. After dinner we were told we could leave the boys there awhile and they would care for them awhile. They kept staying until the family could not give them up and in a couple of years or more, Mr. Marshall wrote that they did not regret taking them and would feel very sorry to have to now give them up. I cannot recall where utter failure was made. Sometimes I had to board a child a few days somewhere or take him or her home with me, but the place opened in some way for a home for the child. How I would like to know the situation of each one now that these years have gone by.

Thomas Demourjin.

SPRING VALLEY, MINNESOTA - FRIDAY, JULY 25th, 1901

Children placed were:

Arthur Blick, aged 9, (placed with T. M. Hagerty of Grand Meadow)

James Boland, aged 15, (placed with Donald McGillivary, Leroy)

Harry Bolzman, aged 11, (placed with C. E. Kemple, Spring Valley)

William Bonfield, aged 10, (placed with Jacob Riel, Spring Valley)

John Clarke, aged 11, (placed with R. W. Terry, Spring Valley)

James Costello, aged 15, (placed with Mrs. M. Taylor, Spring Valley)

Patrick Divine, aged 10, (placed with Fred Wrace, Cherry Grove)

Augusta Heilman, aged 10, (placed with Jacob Devoss, Cherry Grove (See Lime Springs, Iowa distribution)

Emma Heilman, aged 12, (placed with E. A. Jurish, Cherry Grove-See Lime Springs, Iowa distribution)

Willie Johnson, aged 10, (placed with F. L. Wolfgram, Grand Meadow)

Louis Jones, aged 9, (placed with William Bradley, Spring Valley-See also Dodge Center, Minnesota distribution)

August Kaherbeck-Bennett (see also Lime Springs, Iowa distribution)

Harry King, aged 10, (placed with Jas. McGhie, Washington)

Ernest Landberg, aged 9, (placed with Mrs. P. J. Palmer, Washington)

Otto Lassen, aged 13, (placed with Walter Thompson, Monona, Iowa)

Frank Lee, aged 10, (placed with C. J. Loucks, Spring Valley)

Bennie Newman, aged 9, (placed with Jas. Stanton, Wykoff)

Walter Reed, aged 11, (placed with John Bateman, Grand Meadow)

Clarence Whitman, aged 9, (placed with Stillman Benjamin, Spring Valley)

The following article appeared in the *Lanesboro Leader* on Saturday, August 3rd, 1901:

Note: The age of the children and who they were placed with was listed in this article and appears after the names of the children above.

A WORTHY WORK
A New York Society Finds Good
Homes In Fillmore County
For Orphan Children

On Friday of last week 19 orphan children from New York City, ranging in age from eight to 15 years, arrived in Spring Valley for the purpose of finding them suitable homes in the families of the prosperous and liberal hearted people of Southeastern Minnesota. The little ones came in charge of R. M. Brace, a representative of the children's aid society of New York City. This institution has been in existence many years and is supported by contributions from the public. Since its existence many homeless and worthy children have been placed with kind-hearted Christian families. The last shipment into Spring Valley was in 1883 at which time 15 boys of various ages found comfortable homes. The most of them have turned out well and have become citizens that would be a credit to any community.

In the lot that arrived for distribution last Friday 17 of them were boys, and two were little girls. A cleaner, better behaved or more intelligent lot of children would be hard to find. A large gathering of people had assembled at the depot to welcome them. They were taken at once to the armory where refreshments had been prepared for them. The local committee in charge of the arrangements at the Valley were: Rev. E. M. Sutton, pastor of the M. E. church; Rev. W. J. Cook of the U. B. church; Rev. J. A. Jackson, of the Baptist church; Rev. W. A. Warren, of the Congregational church; Messrs. B. F. Farmer, S. L. Olds, D. W. Rathburn, and Geo. L. Fort; Mesdames E. W. Thayer and J. A. Sample. The whole were superintended by Rev. H. D. Clark, of Dodge Center.

Without difficulty the children were all placed and Mr. Brace is highly pleased with the prospects. Those who receive the children agree to keep them until they are 18 years of age to make them members of their families, and to send them to school during the winter until they are 16, and during the winter after that. Later if they want to adopt them they will be allowed to do so. Most of the children in the Spring Valley consignment know but very little of their parents, as they died when they were young.

Mr. Robert N. Brace brought out the children and met me at Spring Valley. A company had once been placed here eighteen years before and all had done so well that their record has us in great favor with the people. So, we had ready applicants. Years after that first company, Mr. Brace wrote me that that company I had arranged for was one of the most successful he had ever placed and he was always gratefully pleased to think of it. Of that former company, I will mention one most remarkable case: A family of immigrants landed at New York City and while getting into the city, a boy was separated from the rest of the family. For some reason, he was not found by them. In time he was received by the Children's Aid Society and placed with a Mr. Farmer of Spring Valley, Minnesota. He was taught to work, given a good education and making a story as short as possible, he became one of Minnesota's prominent educators. He was a member of the State Regents. In 1913 he went to New York to occupy some other prominent position and was at a banquet. While talking there the question of the "lost boy" came up and Mr. Farmer remarked that he belongs to that army. He then told the story of his separation from his parents thirty years before and told the names of his sisters and mother and that he had never heard from them since. The man to whom he was talking at once remarked that he knew a woman by one of those names, whereupon Mr. Farmer went to the telephone and called up the town (Peekskill, N.Y., I think) and asked for that name, and lo!, it was his own sister. He went up and seen her and learned that he had his other sister and mother in Cincinnati, Ohio. The sister being married. I was riding on the street car in Cincinnati when I read the account of this in a daily and I soon called up on the phone the party mentioned (the sister) and inquired about it. I told her I had placed a company myself at Spring Valley and that his record greatly helped in placing the other children. She invited me to come and dine with them on Thanksgiving. This was a remarkable find after so many years of separation. I have assisted boys and girls in finding fathers or mothers or brothers and sisters after years of separation and it was such joy to know of their happiness.

We had seventeen boys and two girls on our July 1901 distribution. We had one very sweet little Catholic girl of about three years and there was no Catholic application for her. We could have placed her in dozens of other good homes. I offered a priest three dollars a day for the time he would take to get a good Catholic family to take her, sending him a stamp for a reply. I never heard from him. She was sent back for some other company. One Catholic boy was placed at Grand Meadow, Minnesota with a Catholic farmer, where he stayed until he was of age.

Willie Bonfield became quite a scholar.

Willie Johnson was a fine singer and promised well, but after a while he had trouble with his foster parents and left them and went his own way for wages here and there. One Italian boy turned out to be almost a desperado.

I will mention one as indicating ingratitude occasionally seen, especially in boys. Frank Lee was placed with a farmer who did fairly well with him at first, but at one time resorted to violence so fearful, knocking him with a pitchfork or barrel stave. I removed him, placing him with this man's brother-in-law. Not long after, he bribed the boy to come back, promising him a pair of colts and a share in the cream checks. Hearing of this, I went to investigate the case. I found the man so threatening and impudent that I told him I should not be talked to that way and should take the boy away unless he now promised before witnesses to give the boy the colts at once, as well as the cream shares, and treat him well. He did. A few years later I received a letter from the long lost mother of the boy, asking where he was. I wrote Frank that I had found his mother and asked if he wanted her address. He replied, "If you have kept me from my mother all these years, I'll make it hot for you." I wrote back, "None of your threats to me my boy. Who took your part when you were pounded with a barrel stave and knocked down? If you want your mother's address, treat me well. I never knew your mother until she wrote to me a few days ago." I gave him her address, but I never heard from him again.

Ernest Lindburg was a Protestant, but a Catholic woman wanted him so much that she promised to send him to a Protestant Sunday School and he went to her and she fulfilled her promise. It was

New York law that Catholic children should be placed with Catholics and Protestants with Protestants. This rule we followed with exceptions that after a Catholic had lost his home, I then would place him with Protestants. It was, as a rule, hard to find good Catholic homes that would take children.

Bennie Newman was born June 25th, 1892. He was a Catholic and was placed with such. After a while the family moved to California, but not adopting Bennie, we would not let him go so far away from our oversight. He was sent back to his aunt in New York City on October 10th, 1904. In a few months they were so homesick for the boy that Mr. Stanton wrote that he'd agree to move back to Minnesota if they could have the boy again. They came and he went and was adopted in 1905.

Clarence Whitman went to a farmer at Spring Valley. Later he asked privilege to take the boy into Northern Minnesota. He went and though we made several efforts to locate him and once hearing he was near Rugby, North Dakota, but we never heard from him again. It was the policy of the Society to keep a constant lookout for all under age who were not legally adopted.

There were quite a number in this company that were quite interesting in history. Following this distribution, I made visits to one hundred eighty children in Minnesota, Iowa, Missouri and Wisconsin. I traveled three thousand six hundred seventy-nine miles by rail and eight hundred fifty-five miles by livery, at an expense of four hundred two dollars and ninety-seven cents. This actually took eighty-seven days, but I charged up only sixty-five days, as I made several stops to see old friends, preaching at Marion, Iowa and Omaha, Nebraska.

(top). James Boland.

(bottom). Willie Bonfield.

(top). Augusta Heilman (back right) with her children.

(bottom). Emma and Ernest Heilman.

(top). Louis Jones.

(bottom). August Kaherbeck

51

Bennie Newman.

KENYON, MINNESOTA - FRIDAY, DECEMBER 6th, 1901

<u>Some children placed were</u>:
Herbert Bram (placed secondly with C. R. Chrislock, Wanamingo,
   Minnesota)
Mary Bock
Charles Heing?
Claude Hoagland (placed with S. K. Haugen)
Annie Johnson
George Lachnaeur
Eugene Lange
Fred Lange
William Lange
Harold Lowe
George L. McPeek
Pauline Miller
Fred Neiman
William Neiman
John Rutland
William Young (placed with Herman Myers)
Charles Young (placed in same home as brother, above)

Mr. B. W. Tice, with whom I was to be associated with more or less in years to come, came with fifteen children, four of whom were little girls. Annie Johnson went to some Swedes.

Mary Bock-Corkham had a strenuous life in different homes. She was a bright, vivacious girl, a little inclined to affection, and fast after the boys. She was placed with a physician, but did not "fit in the home." I removed her to a widow, a Christian woman who loved the girl, but later on felt she must give her up, as she was deceiving her and in great danger morally. I then took her to a family near Rochester, but made the mistake of not inquiring into the religion of the family. I found she was with a Catholic and our rules were not to place a Protestant with such. I told the man that and that if she were a Catholic I would be glad to let her stay. She had united with a Baptist church however. He protested and refused to give her up. He was one of our state legislators and should have known the law, for I could not have taken her away if she chose to stay, being sixteen years of age then. I insisted (though I said nothing about a girl's lawful privilege in Minnesota to choose her own guardian at fourteen years). I used up a dollar and twenty-five cents in telephone fees. I told him I would probably be obliged to send the Sheriff. The next day he phoned and said that, "the angel of peace had come over him and if I would send him twenty-five dollars for clothes he had given her, he would put her on the train for me." I paid them twenty-five dollars for a cloak they had given her (second hand) and she was sent to me, crying. She had some boys that were taking her to dances I supposed, and would have made her wild in a short time. She had already been in doubtful company and made her confession. At last she went to an Adventist florist, as later her sister did too. She was educated in an academy. She married a very fine man and settled in Des Moines, Iowa and is happy and faithful. She once wrote:

"Dear Friend,

I remember you a great many times, and often wonder what I would have done if it had not been for you. I certainly would not be enjoying the pleasures I am having from day to day. I wish I had a great big home to take poor children in to, but as I haven't, I'll have to do the best I can by being thankful that I got in to the home I did and wish I had been there sooner. I remain your little girl that's growing old. M. B. K - " In another letter she wrote, *"It does not seem possible that I've been away from home two years. Your letter was certainly a great help to me, as it happened that day that I was thinking of past times. Why did God have my lot as He did? I can see His great kindness in leading me safely through as He did. It has been a very good year to me as the Lord has been my leader. I thought I'd tell you how much good your letter did me and then you would write me again."*

Herbert Bram was born December 8th, 1892.

Claude Hoagland was very badly abused and I finally sent him to his mother in Canesteo, New York, which brought great joy to she and him. Another of these boys went into a clothing store in Minneapolis. One of the boys, years later, hired out to a drinking man, was taken to a saloon by him. He was drunk one day and ahead of him was a girl in a buggy. He ran into the buggy as he was driving a milk wagon and threw the girl out, breaking her shoulder. He was to be arrested or pay the doctor's bill. He appealed to me for defense and I told him he should not be arrested and he had learned his lesson about drinking and must not taste a drop of beer again, which he promised he would not do. Then I said, "I'll not let you be arrested until the saloon is arrested and all the men who voted for its license are arrested. When they were all under arrest and in jail, then it would be time to arrest a boy who was drunk by consent of the people." They never arrested him. He later went to the Dakotas and wrote me a thankful letter.

George Lachneaur lost his first home and I removed him to Worth McPeek's near Kasson, Minnesota. This was about ten miles from me. He was a sedate, quiet, industrious, honest boy. He is now adopted and owns eighty acres of fine farm land. He is a splendid fellow and greatly loved, almost worshipped by the family, who have no other children. He will be the heir to more farms. In 1925 I visited him at his home near Byron, Minnesota and took pictures of his house and family. When my wife died, he came and sat next to me as one of the family.

Eugene Lange was born July 6th, 1890. He was replaced April 24th, 1905 at Dodge Center, Minnesota. He ran away and went back to Kenyon and then came to me in March 1907. He found work at Skyberg and in 1908 he enlisted at Minneapolis. He went to the Philippines in 1910.

Fred Lange now owns a bakery at Rochester. The other Langes became quite industrious on other avocations. Another went to the Rochester, Minnesota Post Office and earns seventy-five dollars a month. One of these brothers gave me all sorts of trouble, but saved some of his wages and later married and settled down and works at a creamery for good wages.

Harold Lowe was born July 1st, 1893. A fine fellow. He became a merchant.

The most pathetic case in this party of children was a little girl of eight years. Her name was Pauline Miller. She was placed with a family highly recommended, on a farm. In about a year her folks put a few scanty clothes in a gunny sack, put a tag on her, and sent her to me at Dodge Center. I was working in my garden in sight of the railway station when a man came out and called to me to come and get a girl that was there. I took her to my home and later on placed her in another home that was recommended well. I supposed he was living with his wife, but after coming away I found it was his sister and that his wife did not live with him, though she came up from Iowa sometimes to visit him! I then told him that as long as his sister was there to care for the child, she could stay. Later, he wrote me he was married and wanted to take the girl with them to the Dakotas. He went at once, before I could make the investigation. His new wife wrote me all kinds of stuff about her husband and his wrong acts. Before I knew it, he had sent the child to his niece back where he used to live, but there was no one to meet her at the station. The Methodist pastor saw her and took her to the home to which she was sent. The child was almost gone with consumption from her exposure and treatment. The niece at once wrote me to come and get her and send her to New York. I ordered a ticket and went to get her and found that she could not even turn over in bed she was so weak, and the doctor said that she would probably not live the week out. As I entered the sick room, she looked up to me so pitifully and said, "Oh, Mr. Clarke, I don't want to be toted about any more." I replied, "My dear girl, you shall not be any more. You are to have the very best home and stay always." I was speaking of heaven. I went to the undertaker and told him the case and that I might not be there. I wanted him ready with a little casket, but a cheap one. He agreed to do so and in a week she died. The undertaker sent me a bill of fifty-five dollars. I wrote him that I had not agreed to such an expense as that and to cut it in half. He replied that if I did not send the money in a few days, he would sue me. He was paid fifty dollars for his advantage of me.

There was a great funeral. Crowds came to hear about the poor orphan child, and the Society and agent was greatly praised for such tender care and burial. I then wrote the foster father that he must pay the bill under such awful circumstances, for which he was to be blamed. He sent his niece fifty dollars to meet the expenses and she appropriated it all to herself for three weeks care of the child. He parted from his second wife and I received some awful and very peculiar letters from her in regard to his terrible treatment of the child. How much of it was true, I could not say. The dear child died May 1st, 1904. In 1912, after the burial of my wife and in the erection of a monument, I told the story to a man in Rochester, and he said he would place a stone at the child's grave, which he said he did in 1913. I want to visit that little grave sometime.

Charles Young was born March 10th, 1894.

(top left). Marie Bock.

(top right). Herbert Bram.

(bottom). Claude Hoagland.

(top left). Annie Johnson.

(top right). Eugene Lange.

(bottom). Harold Lowe in back, along with his foster brother and his teacher.

George L. McPeek.

Charles and William Young.

PLAINVIEW, MINNESOTA - DECEMBER 4th, 1902

<u>Some children placed were</u>:
August Brenison
Mario Henry Edmond
John Forstman
Benjamin "Dale" Huggard
George Huggard
Thomas Huggard
Henry Schaupy
Carrie Schroeder
Frances Schroeder (see "Guardianships")
Lillian Schroeder
Ina Lillian Stevens
Edna Turk
Frank Turk
Ralph Turk (placed with C. H. Richardson)
Jennie May White
Harry Wright

This was a very successful distribution and a few of the wards I had special care of in an unusual way. The distribution took place at the G. A. R. Hall. There were eight boys and six girls in the company. A Miss Bogardus was the woman assisting. At the close of the distribution, one little Turk boy burst into tears and said, "I want to see my sister." There were two brothers and a sister. He thought she had gone from him forever, but I assured him that she was near by and he would often see her. However, Edna Turk was taken by her foster parents to California and was a shy girl, always fearing I was going to take her away when I made a visit. The mother of these three children died on November twenty-sixth, which was on the birthday of her boy George (and mine as well). The mother, in giving up her boys, said before she died, "I want my boys placed where they will grow up church people." After those years, it looks as though that mother's request would not be fulfilled, except in the case of the girl, for the boys did not do as well as wished. Ralph Turk was born July 26th, 1896.

The Huggard brothers were made motherless the twenty-sixth of November 1902. Just about a month before placing at Plainview. Thomas Huggard was born November 26th, 1890. Benjamin (called "Dale") Huggard was born December 21st, 1893.

Henry Schaupy, who was later on adopted, came to live at Dodge Center.

Carrie and Lillian Schroeder were adopted by a farmer and later went to California and married. They were fine and intellectual girls. The third sister and youngest, Frances Schroeder, became my ward later on.

Ina Lillian Stevens had a checkered career. A pretty girl, but fickle and affected. I placed her several times. Finally, I took her to Iowa where she was placed three times. At last I placed her near Dodge Center and she went to a Nevada, Iowa Sanitarium to study nursing, but could not make it. She then came back and my wife secured her a place for wages and she married the young man in that home and went into Iowa. She left her husband, or he left her, and she worked here and there. I later lost all track of her. She often wrote me appreciative letters and was pleased to call me her truest and best friend. She called on me in August of 1915.

Little Jennie May White, nearly ten years of age, was not taken that day. Her father was Norwegian and her mother was Irish. She came up to me with tears in her eyes and said, "Don't anybody want me?" I told her we would find her a home the next day, which we did, but the poor child seemed to be born for trouble. She had seven pennies someone had given her on the cars or at the Hall, and the foster father borrowed a nickel! Childlike, she was in a hurry for her pay and she stole it from his pocket, and was turned away for it. I replaced her several times. At last she went back to New York and soon was sent to the central part of the state where she had been before coming west. Upon reaching age, she was engaged to be married, but broke the engagement. Still, he wanted to visit her and she wrote asking what was best to do. Soon, she was re-engaged and the day set for marriage, but again it was broken off. Her first foster parents had moved to South Dakota and sent for her to come to them, which she did. In South Dakota, I visited her. Soon she returned to New York and was again engaged to another man. She returned to the Dakotas and he followed her and married her. In a year a sweet little girl came to bless them, but she was unhappy, as he had "taken to drink" and abused her she said. She wanted me to help her, but I advised her to stay by him. They then went to New York state to live near where I used to live, and seemed for a long time to do better. She wrote many letters of appreciation and always signed her name "Your little New York girl." At last, she deserted her husband, taking the child with her, and he wrote me finally that he had located her, the child having died, and I think she may also have died. She went astray.

(top). Benjamin Huggard.

(bottom). Thomas Huggard.

Ina Lillian Stevens and her husband.

Distributions

(top). Ralph Turk.

(bottom). Jenny May White (r).

Distributions

Some children placed were:
George Angus
Harry Bull (placed with Freeman Brown and then Mark Ellis)
Walter Bull (placed with Mark Ellis)
Una Church (placed with William Savidge)
Margaret Dauman
Patrick Divine
Eliza Doran
Edward Kimmerlee
Harry King
Gustave Lindburg
Ethel Melville
Henry Schaupye "Harry Miller" (placed with the Miller family)
Spencer Tingley

This was another fine distribution. There were fifteen children, four being girls. Miss Bogardus was the nurse, assisting in care of girls. Mr. Tice was also with us. Among the wards of this placing:

George Angus went to Preston, Minnesota.

Walter and Harry Bull became successful farmers and went to the World War and returned to Chatfield. Walter was born January 7th, 1891 and Harry on September 9th, 1892.

Una Church was one of the most interesting cases. She was found on a street in New York, abandoned, and was so near "gone" that she could not talk for many days. No one knew her name or nationality or birth date. In coming west with this company, the Yonkers Unitarian Church gave a sum of money to pay her fare and the congregation in Sunday School gave her the name "Una Church" after the Unitarian Church. It is a charity for some people to pay the fares of some certain wards and to hear of them later on for some sweet satisfaction. We gave her the date of placing (January 5th) as her birthday. The year (1896) was guessed at. She still lives at Chatfield last I heard. I have her photograph and have visited her a number of times.

69

Margaret Dauman was a fine girl, also placed near Preston on a farm. She was quite retiring and modest in manner.

Patrick Divine was a very pleasing little boy, and lovable. He went to Preston and was one of the favorites of Mr. Brace at the New York headquarters.

Eliza Doran was not applied for and she went back to Chicago to be boarded until we went to Corydon, Iowa later on. She then was placed there and later I took her to Greenfield, Iowa and in time she went with her foster parents on to Missouri. There she married a young farmer named Earl Sappington and has been ever since an interesting correspondent. On January 1st, 1915 she wrote:

"Dear Mr. Clarke,

You will be surprised to know that I am back to W - Missouri. I had throat trouble and had my tonsils removed. I have been looking for a letter from you for some time, but I know you are very busy answering so many. (I had written one thousand sixty-eight during 1914, but that was half what I used to write in a year). *I received some nice and beautiful presents at Christmas. I am writing to let you know that I am to be married the 3rd of January at three o'clock. We will live in the country four miles from town in our old neighborhood. I will always be glad to hear from you. I am as ever, Lizzie."*

Edward Kimmerlee, a Hebrew, finally ran away from his home.

Harry King was born January 14th, 1891. He was not a steady boy. He married, but did not provide for his wife and child and she would write to me for encouragement.

Gustave Lindburg finally went to Welton, Iowa and made a lot of trouble. He also had two brothers placed elsewhere who were troublesome.

Others were placed that I need to mention. Ethel Melville was a handsome and a very precocious girl. She was very talented and her letters showed much talent in describing scenery. She had a fine home with elderly people who took great pains with her. She would have a "little spat" with them, as she called it, and they would sometimes send for me to come and settle it. When she was, as she said, "sweet sixteen," she sent for me to come and see her. I found her with twinkling eyes and full of mischief. I asked her what was the matter and she replied, "Oh, mamma and I do not always agree and we have had a little spat, but she always begins it."

"Yes," I said, "and you always end it. What is the sense in spats?"

She smiled and asked, "Is a girl at sixteen too young to have some company?"

"That depends. Who is he?," I replied.

"A young man comes to see me and mamma don't care, he is twenty-two and has been a soldier in the Phillippines."

"But that is a rather bad school for a young man," I said.

"But he has no bad habits, does not use tobacco, nor drink, nor use bad language, and he has sent his mother four hundred dollars to help her," she said.

I replied, "That is quite in his favor." "Well, can I have him?," she asked.

"When do you want him?," I asked.

"In a couple of years, he wants me to go to school more," she replied.

"He is sensible," I said.

"But, can I have him?," she asked again.

"Yes, you can have him," I replied.

There was lots of fun in her, and yet a serious tone. He went to business college and she graduated at High School. They are now at Saskatchewan, Canada on a large ranch. Her descriptive powers are wonderful, as she tells of the beauties of the country. The girl is proud of her foster mother and a real comfort to her in her widowhood. She described her wedding in detail, like an authoress. In August of 1914 she wrote:

"Your letter was lost for two months in my box of sandle-wood (I use oriental perfumes) . . . About your not receiving an invitation to our wedding; I was in no way to blame. One day, while sorting out letters, invitations, snap shots, etc., those to take with me and those to burn, I placed yours and some other things on the table to go and meet an engagement and returning I found much to my sorrow, that mother had by mistake burned them and other things I greatly prized. Your address was lost. Although we received

many beautiful presents, none would have been more highly prized than some token of the occasion from you. We had about sixty at the wedding and everything went lovely. About the same number were at the depot and a dozen went as far as Rochester with us. Please forgive me, your letter was certainly a surprise, for it brought up the past that my foster mother and friends have tried to completely banish from my memory. In fact, so well have they accomplished it, that of another home life and blood ties, I never think. Indeed, until your letter came, it was so completely out of my mind that for some moments, I could hardly piece things together. While other girls have had the knowledge of their birth and parentage brought to them in various ways, I never did. To my foster mother, I am hers and the past to her means that in some way it might estrange us, although that is absurd isn't it? In some way, I never cared who I was, where I came from. To me the past is a sealed book and I hate to break the seal. Mother and father means nothing to me. My case is one of 'let the dead bury their dead.' Will drop you a card when I know my future plans. Ethel."

While back in Chatfield on a visit to the old home, she wrote the following:

"I am home and Oh, its simply grand. Seems like old times . . . almost as though I am not married. I'm head over heels in church work, morning and evening . . . choir, double quartet, Sunday school teacher, first Vice President of Epworth League. H - is still in Canada. I expect to go in March. Did you get my history? What work are you interested in now? I feel like having a chat with an old friend. Always glad to hear from you. Mother sends best regards. Ethel" Again, in another letter she wrote: *"I will not call you a flatterer 'cause I know you are sincere in your remarks, but I fear you look out of partial eyes. Yes, I'm sure glad to get back, but sometimes, when I gaze at the hills and trees, I find myself longing for the great northwestern Canadian prairies. Wouldn't you like to be where you could know all of nature's melodies . . . the prairie song, the woodland hymn, the sob of the sea, the echoes of mountains, all of them? I like everything but a rainy day. I've got your kid-tea-party with Emma. Nice job you have writing history. I could never get one*

pieced together. My history? Yes, write it, but keep it until I call for it. Somehow I hate to dig it up, but look it up and write it and then let me know. It will seem almost like a strangers. Sometime come and see us. Sincerely, as of old, Ethel."

Henry Schaupy was added to the company from Plainview, Minnesota. He was born August 2nd, 1898. He killed some flies in his home and they thought he was so cruel that they turned him off and I replaced him. He was a good boy, but he nor the family had come to learn that flies were disease breeders.

Spencer Tingley had a grandmother who claimed she was his guardian and had never surrendered him and after some troublesome negotiations, he was sent back to his folks.

Some of the boys from this company served in the army during the late war with Germany. In fact, from almost every company there were those who went into the army or navy, when old enough.

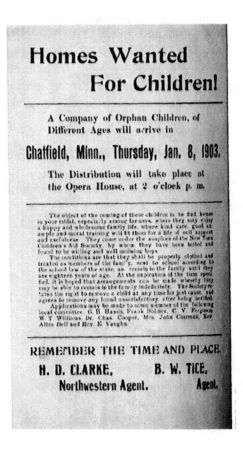

Dodger for the Chatfield, Minnesota company of January 8, 1903.

Walter (back right) and Harry Bull (front right), along with their friends, Walter
and Louis Finley.

(left). Una Church.

(below). Eliza Doran and husband.

(top). Ethel Melville.

(bottom). Henry Schaupye.

Harry King.

CORYDON, IOWA - FEBRUARY 12th, 1903

Some children placed were:
Blanch Caney
Louis Caney
Lizzie Doran (see also Chatfield, Minnesota distribution)
Daniel George (placed with H. J. Haney of Humeson, Iowa)
Bertha Harris "Ruth Hook"
Elizabeth Hickey (see "Guardianships")
Boy-LaVigne
Boy-LaVigne
Willard LaVigne
Ernestine Newbert (placed with Dr. D. D. Drennan)
Agnes Skogland (placed with Warren H. Burton)
Ethel Skogland "Helen Palmer" (placed with Peter V. Palmer of
  Humeston, Iowa)
Ivan Skogland (placed with Dr. B. S. Walker)
Carrie Waupak

This was also an interesting and very successful distribution. Mr. B. W. Tice was to bring the children from New York. His business being chiefly to bring parties west after picking them out in the city. He had been Superintendent of one of the Boy's Lodging Houses previous to this. He was a large fleshy man, genial countenance, fine looking and very cheerful, but his health was quite poor at this time and continued to be so until he died about 1911. Miss Anna Laura Hill, of Elmira, N.Y., was the nurse for the little ones and girls. Miss Hill often accompanied both Mr. Tice and myself on trips west. I was to have been with this company, but was sent elsewhere, as I will presently relate. I think there were about fifteen of these. I did have oversight of these wards after placing.

Louis and Blanch Caney gave me some trouble to keep them in a home. I placed them near each other. Due to illness in one home and moving to the "coast" and "selling out" by the other family, I had to place them both together in a home in eastern Iowa. Mr. Stotler was the foster father. They were separated again however. Blanch was a beautiful child and affectionate. She was taken to Iowa City Hospital for an operation and finally married near Corydon, where she was first placed. Louis, her brother, did not do as well and went about "from pillar to post."

Mentioning some of these, before my trip to Texas at this date . . . Lizzie Doran mentioned in the Chatfield company was with us here, where she found a temporary home. Lizzie was born January 6th, 1893.

Daniel George was born March 11th, 1899.

Bertha Harris "alias Ruth Hook" was born June 5, 1895. She came from Elmira, New York.

Ernestine Newbert was born January 27th, 1897.

Willard LaVigne became a marine and was with Uncle Sam a long time. The LaVigne twins were replaced.

Of one Swede family named Skogland there were two sisters and a brother. The brother, Ivan, was a very fine boy. He was born December 22nd, 1898. He was taken by a physician to Texas, but he died of tuberculosis three years later. Agnes Skogland "Dagner Agnes" was born September 6th, 1891. She went with a family to New Mexico and married a ranchman and merchant. She was age twelve when taken and was later legally adopted. She has been a fine little wife and mother ever since. Another brother, Arthur, came to Cumberland, Iowa later on and developed a roving disposition and a bad temper. Three years after this distribution, I brought the sister Ethel to Corydon, who was adopted in 1912 as Helen Palmer by a family of that name. She was born May 24th, 1896. She went to her sister Agnes in San Jon, New Mexico and then returned to Humeston. She was a very vivacious girl of six years, active and affectionate, and I had a long correspondence with her until her marriage to Harry Biggs of Galesburg, Illinois. At this writing, she is in Chicago at work. She always seemed to almost regard me as a father, though she had a good home and foster parents. This was one peculiarity of many of these children who were not legally adopted, for they knew that there was a possibility of their losing their homes in some way and that I was to see about it and look after their welfare.

Carrie Waupak went to College at Des Moines (Drake University).

(top). Bertha Harris.

(bottom). Elizabeth Hickey.

(top). Daniel George with
two foster sisters.

(bottom). Ernestine Newbert

Left to right: Ivan, Ethel and Agnes Skogland.

Carrie Waupak (r) .

CELESTE AND ALVARADO, TEXAS - FEBRUARY, 1903

Some children placed at Alvarado were:
John Beller (replaced at Keene, Texas)
Martin Beller
Walter Bennet, (age 11)
Joseph Brown (from Utica, New York Orphan Asylum, age 5)
Paul Hasler (age 17)
Johnnie Johnson (age 13)
Oscar Kock (age 4)
Edward Mackey (not of my company, but came from Pilot Point, Texas)
Lewis Osterhandt (age 13)
Herbert Ponton (age 16, died of pneumonia soon after placing)
Dennis Regan (old enough to look after himself very soon)
Charles Smith (soon looked after himself)
Nathan Strencher (soon looked after himself and went back to New York)
Walter Tobisen (age 15)

Children placed in or near Celeste were:
George Cody (with S. H. Culver, Kingston)
Charles Deacon (with W. L. Duke, Leonard)
Edward Gross (with W. R. Clark, Celeste)
Maurice Homan (with F. A. Hudson, Honey Grove)
Frederick Jelliff (formerly with T. C. Clark, now with Pate Taylor, Celeste)
Arthur Jerolamon (with R. M. Harris, Celeste)
Michael Kreitchen (with Joseph Simmons, Celeste)
Valentine Moran (with Mrs. I. D. Webb, Wolfe City)
Eddie Miller (with D. A. Edwards, Celeste)
Harry Reid (formerly with J. R. Watson, now with J. H. Miller, Celeste)
James Sayers (formerly with John Harbert, Celeste, now with P. C. Clarke, Leonard)
Joseph Wood (with A. R. Miller, Celeste)

Henry Wood (formerly with M. V. Moore, now with V. C. Cole, Celeste)

David Taylor (with Arthur Averitt, Leonard-left his home without consent-age 16)

In the month of February in 1903, I was sent to Texas with Mr. Brace, having twenty-seven boys and two girls. I left home on the ninth of February for Saint Louis, Missouri. Mr. Brace telegraphed me at Saint Louis that they were late and for me to hold the train until they reached there. It was to start for Los Angeles, a through train, and did not usually wait for incoming trains. We divided them in Texas into two companies. I had charge of fourteen boys. Brace went to Celeste and I to Alvarado. Enroute, the company ran out of provisions and I held up the train, and in St. Louis I bought fifteen dollars worth of eats and boarded the train. Before we reached our destination we were again out of food and at Paris, Texas I again replenished the stock, having to get it inside of ten minutes.

One of the strangest hotel meals I ever ate in twenty minutes was in a wooded town or feeding place, then in the north east corner of Indian Territory. I had become so tired of sandwiches on the train and had eaten no breakfast to speak of and Mr. Brace said, "You rush out and eat and I'll stay with the children." I was quickly seated at a table and saw this announcement on a card by my plate that read, "This menu served in the following order." A girl stood near and began to serve me, whether I wanted it or not. I received potatoes and dressing, pork steak, beef steak, chicken, hash, venison, bread of different kinds and butter, coffee, vegetables, fruits, pudding, pies, cakes, cheese, etc. , etc. The grand final total was seventy-five cents and I rushed for the train!

When the train stopped at Farmersville, Texas, a station enroute, we lost a boy. It was a usual thing that passengers were interested in our children and would give them pennies or nickels and take them in their laps. It seems a man, perhaps drunk, had one of the boys, and when he got off at Farmersville he took the boy with him and we never noticed it until the train had gone far. Mr. Brace telegraphed to me, as he had gotten off at his place of distribution. The

Conductor had seen the man take the boy and called to the station agent as the train was moving out to get the boy, which he did and sent him on the next train.

Our two girls, who were sisters, had already been spoken for. One by an Episcopal Rector and the other by a Dr. Martin at Bonham, Texas. The doctor took the one that was somewhat cripple and in time, by proper treatment, she was almost fully healed. We placed all the boys quite successfully. I put up at the Commercial Hotel at Alvarado kept by Mrs. Haltecote. All hotels I stayed at were kept by women and I traveled in many towns. At my distribution I was at first greatly discouraged, as there was only one woman in the opera house. The rest were all men, filling the room with blue tobacco smoke, but Texas furnished many many homes for boys that seemed to be well cared for. My distribution took place on February 13th, 1903. Mr. Brace did the same at Celeste.

I had a sad scene in placing two brothers much attached to each other, but had to be separated. How one clung to me with almost a death grip, crying for his brother. I assured the brothers that they would meet each other sometimes. One man, evidently to test me, said, "Can I teach the boy to smoke?"

"No sir," I said.

"Can't I take him into the Saloon?"

"No, sir."

"Can't I swear at him?"

"No, sir."

I forgot whether he took the boy or not. These Texans are as a rule, kind hearted men, and usually treated the boys well, though moral standards in Texas are not as high as in the north, save in virtue.

Giving boys away to homes reminded me of the old slave market in the south during the fifties, but with a far different result. No boy was sold. While at Alvarado, there was what is called a "norther," very cold and snowy. The mud was so deep that I could not do the usual visiting right after the placing. On the night of the fifteenth I slept under wooling blankets, three quilts and a spread and my overcoat, and shivered all night with cold. I caught a severe cold that lasted me all the rest of the winter or longer. The local paper gave a glowing account of the placing and told of city conditions and the great work of the Society and the grand results to the homeless children. But for its length, I would copy the article.

The roads were so fearful that the liveryman did not want to drive about for me to see the children, and my wife being at Hammond, Louisiana with Charles and my daughter Mabel; I went there and stayed until March third, and then returned north and my wife came to Chicago and met me. We then returned home.

In June and July that year, I went back and in one month, replaced about twenty boys who had or were to lose their homes. I took one boy to St. Louis and then I returned him to New York City for moral treatment. I visited at that time our little Janette Martin at Bonham, staying a week to have mail caught up, as I was traveling about in a circle to look after the boys in the state. Enroute, I had stopped on a Sabbath at St. Louis and preached at the Seventh Day Adventist church and was well entertained. On one Sabbath I was at Keene, Texas, speaking there and looking at their school and a small orphanage. The orphanage was supported entirely by the earnings of one blind man who simply went about selling the sketch of his life. I had one boy there in a Seventh Day Adventist home by the name of Cleckner. I had one Russian boy named Nathan, who later concluded that he did not want Texas and went back east. There were three boys "at sea" that I put on a train at Fort Worth and sent to a Mr. Reck at Claude, Texas, in the Pan Handle. He was a state agent. Two ran away the next day, one returning part way back and one coming back where I was. As he was seventeen years old, I told him he was old enough to now work his way through life. His name was John. He said he was not going to stay up in the Panhandle with wolves and coyotes! The little girls, Daisy and Juliette, were doing nicely and were in the same city, but later the minister moved to another parish. I visited Celeste, Rockwell, Lancaster, Keene, Alvarado, Garland, Leonard, Bonham and Whitesboro. I dined one day with a Confederate Soldier, at his request. I asked him how it looked to him, these years since the Civil War. "It's all right," he said. "I'm glad the slave is freed, but we can't forget the terrible carpet-bag government that was placed over us."

On this summer Texas trip, I had to go over the ground twice, going about in a circle for a month. I stopped one week at a hotel to let my mail catch up with me. It would seem that twenty boys were on a strike (or the homes were) and that one or both were poor material. It might indicate that the very best of the children were reserved for northern homes, and yet there are very fine homes in the south. Though it was probably true that the very best wards were saved for northern homes, these were an average lot. There were few girls placed in the south, nearly all were boys. I have little sympathy with the cry of "slum children, "low birth," "inevitably predisposed," and all that. I notice that heredity, folly and sin are about the same everywhere. There are so many of our so-called "respectable homes" that produce boys who learn to smoke and swear, be loose in principle, leave the Sabbath they were brought up to observe, and do other things like "foreigners" and "hobos." And while they do them, they boast of purer blood and more refined homes. The best thing to do in any child of any "blood" is to "train him in the way he should go." That is environment and religious education and example. A child is a gift of God and as such must be taught reverently of God and sacred things. "Give the boy a chance," whether legally or illegally born, no matter what color or nationality, or place of birth, he is a precious bundle of love and will become what he later on sees and hears. If "blood tells," better homes tell.

On this trip, the Wabash and the "KT" railway companies issued passes for me. For seven years the Chicago and Milwaukee Railway gave me a pass annually for all their system, as far as Nebraska and North Dakota. Destinations beyond to the west, they did not provide for. Mr. Miller, the C.M. & St. Paul Gen. Pas. Agent, was very kind to me, issuing the passes annually and giving me free telegraphing at any station on his road to ask for special tickets for children or needy ones in our care. We were charged one quarter fare for those of five to twelve, and half fare for all older. The free passes saved hundreds of dollars for charity and also enabled me to go home much oftener than I otherwise would. I could go on the C.M. and Saint Paul road to many points and then transfer to other roads for a short distance.

Mr. Brace visited the state the next year and said my boys had all done unusually well. On the February trip I went over into Louisiana (Hammond) to see Charles and Mabel and my wife, who had gone there for her health for part of the winter, but it was a hard damp winter for the south and she was made worse by it. I met her in Chicago on my journey back to Dodge Center, Minnesota and took her home.

From observation, I think very many foster parents were too exacting and required men's work of boys and women's work of girls. A frequent complaint and cause for removal of a child was that he or she did not like to work. Now, there are some things I never liked to do, and one was milking. I never was in childhood, very enthusiastic about hard work. I did like to play, but I have more than made up for it these late years. Often a man would say, "That boy does not earn his salt." The boy referred to had plowed thirty-five acres of land that spring for corn. He harrowed it and planted it and was doing a man's work. He was one reaper when I visited him. I took him away as requested. Of course, there were some lazy boys and girls as are seen in people's own homes. I placed one boy who laid down on the ground to weed beets and onions. I placed a boy in western Iowa who was homely as a "hedge fence" and very illiterate. He has written me hundreds of letters, all of them being about the same illiterate stuff. BUT, he was industrious and saved his wages, never married, but had a bank account and built himself a house of his own. He was a steady plodder at any work he could find. I suspect by his name he is a Jew, but he farmed a great deal, which is not the usual trade for an American Jew. It is not likely that any woman would ever fall in love with him, but she might do very much worse in marrying a fascinating, handsome, polite hat-doffing dude.

There were lazy boys and girls, but right management and inducements for work will in most cases serve the ward to do his share. Too great indulgence, and letting shiftlessness get possession of one, as well as too much hard work, is cause for dislike of it. Childhood is for play, study, and a moderate amount of chores that are expected daily and regularly. It is a time of preparation. In a way, children are colts and kittens and the mothers look on and enjoy their frolics. In the case of the colt, it has to be "halter-broke." It chafes a bit at first, but working with the older horse, it is soon broken in. Fathers who cheerfully work along side of the boy, and mothers who go into the kitchen with the girl, do not as a rule have very much difficulty. There is some industrial slavery outside of factories. It has been observed on many a farm, but not as a rule where the parents are intellectual and have a love for good books and plays and see something besides work and money for the family. There is no dearth of holidays now, but many years ago the average farmer boy had circus day, July fourth and Christmas, and a day at the county fair. If he went out evenings between those holidays, it was to a husking bee, where he worked all the evening for the privilege of drinking some cider and eating apples and playing "snap-and-catchum," a strenuous kissing game. There were exceptions. Why is it that more girls have been graduated from High School than boys?   Plowing and corn picking is mostly responsible for that. That work has to be done, but shall it be at the everlasting expense of the boy's education?   The boy today without a good High School education is handicapped all his life for a paying position and for happy marriage.

Then, too, I have observed that the kind farmer who gave the boy a calf or pig "for his own" and stuck to his bargain, and the family that gave the girl some chickens, not using up the money for the family, hardly ever had occasion to complain of a laxy ward or discontented one. "Johnny's calf and dad's cow" has ruined many a boy and took all the ambition out of him. A man in the east gave a boy all the potatoes he could raise on some nice ground beside the road and he worked hard and raised a fine crop and sold them and then used the money himself. That boy lost all ambition and amounted to little after that.

On October thirteenth of that year, Mr. B. W. Tice came to Minnesota and we went together to Saint Paul to consult the State Board of Control to see if we could get the same terms for placing children that Iowa and other states gave us. The board had previously made some decisions in regard to keeping out these orphan wards. We were received very bluntly when courtesy should have been extended, even though our requests were not granted. Later we had a bond of one thousand dollars to the state for protection of wards brought in to that state. That same month I visited all the Minnesota wards, except for two towns, and returned to Nebraska. While in Nebraska I received a letter from an Iowa ward pleading for me to come at once and rescue her from the temptations of a foster father, whose wife had gone to St. Paul on a visit and left the girl to keep the house, etc. She was about fourteen years old. She wrote, "Come quick. I do not want to do anything wrong." I left Nebraska at once and flew on the wings of the fastest trains I could get and arrived there on September sixteenth. She had her clothes all packed and was ready for me to get her. The man slunk off to the barn, his wife having returned, but no harm was done the girl, though the wife blamed her husband. At W-U, I came near placing her with a merchant, but the grandmother of the home was so jealous, thinking her daughter would think more of the girl than of her, they decided not to take her. Afterwards, I was glad, for they left the store for a hotel. I took her home with me for three months and then found for her a good farm home, where she grew up industrious and a help in the church, and a leader of song in the Sabbath School for five years. When a young woman, she was to have been married and the time set, but the faithless fellow went off and married another girl without letting her know it. This was a great blow to the girl and aroused great indignation in the community where she was. I was asked by people there to sue him for breach of promise and one wanted him turned out of a certain organization of which he was a member, but I'd have nothing to do with that. I stood by the girl and made enemies by it. She was a strong girl and a rusher in housekeeping, and would have made a loving helpful wife. Later on another seducer of her church ruined her prospects and in sorrow, she sent for me to come and bury her dead, which I did. At last, she became a trained nurse and was much loved by those who worked with her at that profession in the hospital. Her sister had written me a few years previous to this and asked if she could come and find work near her sister. I had placed her as well. She came and I secured work for her and soon she married a nice young man in the town.

GREENFIELD AND CUMBERLAND, IOWA - APRIL 16th & MAY 16th, 1903

<u>Some children placed were:</u>
Gladys Clement (age 2)
Minnie Fleischaner (replaced with George Speis of Cumberland)
Nelson Fleming (placed later, several times)
Adolphina "Dorotha" Jacobson
Emma Jacobson
Boy-Jewel
LaVigne Twins
Oscar Schultz
Bessie Valentine-Earl (age 2, placed with I. T. and Lillian Earl)
Guy Valentine (placed later in Missouri)
Morris Valentine (placed with L. E. Gile, replaced with S. J. Smith)
Raymond Valentine (placed with John S. Smith)
Willis Valentine (placed later in Missouri)
Joe Vetter (placed in Anita, Iowa)
Charles Vetter (see also Dodge Center, Minnesota distribution)

A very successful distribution and with many fine children. We had a pair of French twins and two other brothers of theirs. The twins were parted soon by removals a thousand or two miles apart and one older brother, after various ups and downs, became one of the navy in the war with Germany. He is now settled in one of the Pacific states. One boy had uncles who were millionaires. One of whom was an official of the Denver and Rio Grande Railway. The boy's father had been "the black sheep" of the family and when he died and left this boy, the uncles would do nothing for him. "Place him" they said. He was a good little boy, but not well, and after a while he had to be sent back for treatments. The New York Hospital treated our wards free and saved many a life.

One very active girl, most precocious and yet there was something very winning and lovely about her. She had one or two trials and I took her into Nebraska, where they had much trouble with her and yet clung to her and did wonders for the child. Some very quaint letters from her and her foster parents would make a story book. At one time they sent her off to a Catholic School with the foolish notion that it would discipline and save her, a very dangerous thing to do and a great fallacy on the part of Protestants. Fearful harm has been done to youth in such schools and there have been cases where they never returned to their homes again or ever heard from.

One of the Greenfield girls I had great trouble with, but mostly from her home, where they worked her "nearly to death" and tried to rob her of her schooling. I had a furious time with the family (Germans) and after several attempts to remove her and the family consulting lawyers, I had her secretly pack her satchel and take them to a neighbors until I came and she waited for me. I hastily arrived, got her into the carriage and rushed to the train. I took her to Brooklyn, Iowa. Again, I had a terrible time to get her from another home and I was threatened with terrible violence, but I secured her again and placed her for wages. She has never written me but once since then. I hear about her occasionally by way of her sister, who was adopted and grew up in her nice home and finally married well.

Gladys Clement was a baby of two years and she was not kept by those who took her in Cumberland. She was born January 12th, (1899)? She had cried so and took on that a nurse had to stay the night with her. The next day she was brought back to us and replaced with a woman that was not nervous and had more tact. After replacing, the man who first took her came and offered us fifty dollars in gold if he could have her back, but we were not selling babies and it was too late anyway. The Children's Aid Society wrote in 1914 that her real last name was Sidney and she had three sisters named Alice, Edith and Lucy. Their father was a clerk. When later the foster father died, his wife and the child were left nearly destitute. She tried hard to get an education so as to support herself and "mamma." She too was finally married well to a Mr. McCurdy of Cumberland, Iowa in February 1916. There seems to be a mistake in her date of birth, as she is not four years old in the picture.

Minnie Fleischaner was placed at Bridgewater from the Greenfield company and in a few weeks, while we were passing through on the cars, the foster mother had her at the station and put her aboard the cars with our other company and would give no reason except, "She does not fit in to our family." Another lady told us that the foster mother was jealous of her husband and would not let the child speak to him. She was then some past eight years of age. The next home educated her and she was very proficient in music, playing the piano well. She married December 22nd, 1915 to Glenn Engle and went to Aberdeen, South Dakota on June 6th, 1925. They have one son.

Nelson Fleming was born August 30th, 1895. He was placed again in 1907 or 1908, and again July 22, 1910. He graduated from High School in 1915 and engaged in YMCA work in Chicago in 1916 and Chatauqua work in 1917. He became a soldier at Camp Custer in Michigan in 1918 with the 255 Ambulance, 14th Sanitary Train. He visited me at Battle Creek, Michigan on July 4th, 1919, while at Camp. He married in Los Angeles, California and resides on 830 W. 42nd Street.

Bessie Valentine was born June 20th, 1900. She married at Red Oak, Iowa to George E. McConkey of Corning. They have one child. Bessie has three brothers; Gay Willis, Raymond and Morris and two sisters; Elizabeth and Flossie of Wolcott, New York. Raymond was born October 16th, 1893. He moved to Sedalia, Missouri in 1910. Morris Valentine was born January 23rd, 1895. He was replaced in February 1904 with S. J. Smith and moved to Dresdon, Missouri.

Charles Vetter was born January 14th, 1895. His parents were separated. He went to Atlantic, Griswold, Manilla and Mapleton, Iowa and finally to Frank Brown in Dodge Center, Minnesota on February 23rd, 1905.

Joe Vetter was born March 19th, 1894. He was replaced and had quite a little trouble, but I held him to his place and when he became a chauffeur years later he wrote me, thanking me for holding him from his madness and self-willed ways. He said he did not know what would have become of him if I had given him up. He later on came to visit me at Dodge Center, Minnesota in 1915.

On February sixteenth I was at Sutton, Nebraska and then took three children to New York City. One of these was a boy who had been left for boarding at the Child Saving Institute and he had raised a hatchet on one of the Institute boys and they would not receive any of our wards temporarily after that.

HOMES WANTED
FOR CHILDREN

A company of Orphan Children
of different ages will arrive in

Greenfield, Thurs., April 16

The distribution will take place at the
Opera House, at 11 o'clock a. m.

The object of the coming of these children is to find homes in your midst, especially among farmers, where they may enjoy a happy and wholesome family life, where kind care, good example and moral training will fit them for a life of self support and usefulness. They come under the auspices of the New York Children's Aid Society, by whom they have been tested and found to be well meaning and willing boys and girls.

The conditions are that they shall be properly clothed and treated as members of the family, sent to school according to the school law of the state, and remain in the family until they are eighteen years of age. At the expiration of the time specified it is hoped that arrangements can be made whereby they may be able to remain in the family indefinitely. The society retains the right to remove a child at any time for just cause, and agrees to remove any found unsatisfactory after being notified.

Applications may be made to some member of the following local committee: J. E. Darrah, E. E. Warren, H. N. Linebarger, Dr. Elmer Babcock, Geo. Potter, Edwin Piper, Mrs. J. A. Griswold, Mrs. David Kirk.

**If the children are not all taken at 11 a. m.
an adjourned meeting will be held at 1:30 p. m.**

REMEMBER THE TIME AND PLACE.

H. D. CLARKE
STATE AGENT

B. W. TICE
AGENT

Dodger for the Greenfield, Iowa company of April 16, 1903.

Gladys Clement and her foster mother.

(top). Minnie Fleischaner (r).

(bottom). Nelson Fleming.

Adolphina Jacobson in 1909 at age twelve.

Emma Jacobson.

(top). Oscar Schultz.

(bottom). Bessie Valentine with husband and child.

Raymond (l) and Morris Valentine (r).

Charles Vetter. Photo taken in November 1911.

AUDUBON, IOWA - JUNE 25th, 1903

Some children placed were:
Cecil Denny
Eddy Denny
Arthur Erickson
Frank Erickson (twin boy)
George Erickson (twin boy)
Henry Hastedt
Mary Hastedt (replaced February 20, 1905 with Herman Rinemund
   and renamed Florence Rinemund)
Carrie Reuber (placed with Mrs. Frank Herndon)
Caroline Strobel (placed with E. N. Taggert)
May Troy

A town named after the famous Audubon, the friend of the feathered tribe and animals. Here a pair of twins were placed with the last name of Erickson. Frank Erickson was born about 1897. I sent one boy back to New York with his father. He was a fine little fellow and I felt sorry to let him go back.

Also, a fine boy by the name of Eddy Denny and his sister Cecil. His sister Cecil remained and often wrote me some excellent letters. She wrote the following letter (in part) on September 10th, 1914:

"After a long time I will write you again . . . I have been dreaming about you. I hope you are all right. My husband and I and baby are going to have some pictures taken and we'll send you one. Lovingly your friend, Cecil."

She was not quite satisfied with her home and they did nothing for her when she was of age and married. She has been very happy in her own home with her husband and three children since then. At one time, when in her foster parent's home, she pled with me while visiting her, "Oh, Mr. Clarke, do take me away, do please," but letting her stay a while longer, she became more satisfied and remained until married. It was hard to resist the weeping pleadings of some children when things were wrong and usually it resulted in removal, but sometimes I

106

thought it better for them to remain. Cecil was born March 19th, 1895. She married R. E. Carley on March 26th, 1913. They have four children and live in Audubon.

There was Mary and Henry Hastedt, who had another sister in Nebraska. Mary was a sweet girl and was renamed Florence Rinemund. She was born May 1st, 1897.

Carrie Reuber was a red haired girl and was placed in a good home. She was born March 19th, 1897. Later, the foster mother was sick and thought she could not keep her and her husband gave the child over to one of our local committeeman, a lawyer, without my knowledge or consent. Six months later I went to visit her and found she had been placed with a man and wife of none too good character and their boys would have been her ruin had she stayed. The first foster mother had recovered and was mourning the loss of the child. I said to her, "You shall have her" and I went after her and was insulted and threatened with violence by the man of the home. I explained the situation to him and told him that he did not have her legally. Carrie was undecided as to what she wanted, but I did not consult the child, only her best interests. I took out my watch and said, "I'll give you just five minutes to get her clothes for me and then there will be something doing." He went after her clothes, swearing at me, and I carried her off and gave her back to her first home. There she grew to womanhood, graduated High School and became a teacher. She was very good in music.

Caroline Strobel was born in 1892. She has a brother Eddie at Wartburg Orphanage, Mount Vernon, New York. She was taken sick in 1908 with tuberculosis "consumption" and I visited her. She died a happy Christian, committing herself to Jesus. A sister came from the east to see her and then stayed and married in the area.

May Troy, an Irish girl of much beauty. She was born July 6th, 1893. She was one time quite disobedient, but never really disagreeable. After her foster father died I had to remove her for things that were not worth the mention. In this watchcare of her she became greatly attached to me and seemed to depend upon my advice and counsel very much, she being too old to really feel like the child of the new home, but they did well by her and she had a fair education and new home, but they did well by her and she had a fair education and went after a while to one of the pacific coast states (Idaho I believe). She became a nurse, studying at Butte, Montana and then married a merchant clerk named F. J. Moidek on June 26th, 1913. She writes me beautiful letters, nearly always signing her name "Your black eyed little girl, Mae." She sent me several pretty pictures of herself and family. At one time, I received a letter most pathetic, as she was feeling that it might be possible that her husband might leave her on finding she was possibly keeping back some of her history, which even she herself did not know well. Possibly, he would not love her after that. She wanted me to tell her who and what her people were, no matter what. I wrote her and told her never to be troubled over that, and that her husband, being an honorable man, would love her for what she was and not for what her parents might possibly be. It appears that no real trouble ever came from it. She writes me annually and has a pretty girl who has commenced to write to "Grandpa Clarke."

Railroad Pass used by Reverend Mr. Clarke for the year 1904.

Cecil Denny with husband and children.

(top). Henry and Mary Hastedt.

(bottom). Carrie Reuber.

Caroline Strobel.

Mae Troy.

NEW SHARON, IOWA - JANUARY 29th, 1904

Some children placed were:
Harry Dicting
William Dicting
Elizabeth Eagen
Blanche Heintz
George Heintz
Matilda Heintz
William Holman (placed with W. W. Swartz)
Ida Johnson
Charles Kimmel
William Mansfield
Samuel Picelle-Thompson (placed with V. P. Welch, Chicago, Illinois)
Ira Shongo
Louis Zucco
Thomas Zucco

Child placed later:
Bessie Cocoran

     On the eleventh of January 1904, I started for Alfred Station, New York to visit my daughter Mabel and family, Charles being pastor there, coming from the Hammond, Louisiana pastorate. From thence, I went on to New York City after a company of boys and girls to take to New Sharon, Iowa, having previously arranged for it. I had rooms at 442 West 23rd Street, called "The Babies Mission." Gathering up a company of six nationalities, i. e. Irish, Hebrew, Swede, Italians, Germans and Americans. We had our pictures taken on the street in a snowstorm on the twenty-second. I had no nurse or helper on this trip, the Superintendent saying I was equal to the emergency!

     This was such an interesting lot of kids and so many of them became especially interested in me later on, that I will give all their names and a few I placed there later on. There were four girls and ten boys. We left New York on Tuesday, January twenty-sixth.

The journey to New Sharon was in a terrible blizzard and we were twenty-four hours late to Chicago. I telegraphed to have the meeting at the Opera House postponed from Thursday morning until Friday morning. Reaching Grinnell, where a change of cars was necessary, I found one hotel in the city of about ten thousand people and it had four beds not engaged. The landlady wanted four dollars for them. The regular price then for commercial travelers was fifty cents each. I declined them at that price. I had not planned to undress the kids, but to lay them dressed on the beds with a coverlet over them so that they would be all ready to quickly go to the train in the morning. We stayed in the depot all night, or until five a.m. and the boys who seemed to straggle about the depot, went out to livery stables and brought in robes and blankets for the kiddies to sleep on. We reached New Sharon when it was ten degrees below zero. The ladies of the town had arranged for us to stop at a private boarding house (Mrs. Sheridan's) for breakfast and rest, paying the expenses. If my memory serves me well, we had about fifty applications for these few children, and though it was such a freezing day, the Opera House was packed full. We had a very fine local committee.

Elizabeth Eagen was a very nice Irish girl. She made good in her home, moved to Kansas and married Leonard McCune of Wichita. He went to the World War and was in the Forty-first Infantry-Tenth Infirmary Medical Corps. Elizabeth's brother James also enlisted.

George Heintz was born July 24th, 1897. His father was Alexander and his mother, Grace. He was from the Five Points House of Industry in New York, being received by the Children's Aid Society on January 14th, 1904. He became a soldier at Fort Logan, Honolulu, Arizona and was discharged. He married and lived on a farm where I placed him. Matilda Heintz was born June 20th, 1894. She was the oldest sister, was a small girl and was lacking in education, so that she could never go in to society, or be more than a faithful hired girl, but such will have their reward. She is living an "old maid" life, a good stand-by as housekeeper for many who need her. She has been hospitalized several times. Blanch Heintz was born May 16th, 1895. She was the younger sister. She grew up, graduated High School on May 19, 1916 and attended Hiland Park College and married Jim

Mitchel of Des Moines, Iowa. I visited her October 21st, 1925 at Des Moines, Iowa, after which they moved to California.

Willie Holman was born October 3rd, 1890. He was the son of a man who was with the famous Sousa's band. Traveling all over the world, he could not or would not care for his boy. Willie was a fine singer and he often stood on street corners in the great city with an outstretched hand and received as much as three dollars at a time. He never did well in school and was rather rough when he grew up.

Ida Johnson was born November 15th, 1899. Her parents were Swedish Protestants   named John and Mary Johnson. She was committed to the Children's Fold on May 18th, 1902 and to the Children's Aid Society in June 1902. Her foster parent died and I removed her to Osceola, Iowa in July 1905 where she grew up a very industrious girl, graduated from High School, became a teacher and married well to a farmer named J. H. Daniels on February 5th, 1921.

William Mansfield had a drunken father, but a good step mother and sister, upon whom I called. The boy said he would "go west with us or run away." The stepmother at last signed the papers surrendering the boy to the Society. He was not contented however and went back to New York in a year or two.

Samuel (Picelle) Thompson was named after the street in New York on which he was picked up. He was born January 23rd, 1896. On the way from Chicago, this man, a merchant, saw him and wanted him. I informed him that I never gave children to strangers until a committee had recommended him or he had furnished good references. He said, "Reserve the boy for me and I'll send you plenty of them." Securing these references, I went with the boy to Chicago and placed him. He thought a great deal of the boy and said, " There is not a fault in him." Of course, I knew of some faults. He renamed him "Robert Welch." In two years (Fall 1907) the father of the boy found him and took him away and the foster parents blamed the Society and me in very strong language. I heard that the father took him, along with his sister to Sacramento, California.

On the ninth I returned to New Sharon to visit the wards as placed. This was a very successful placing and many of them turned out unusually well. Two of the girls were taken later on to Kansas by foster parents. They were bright and helpful girls and stayed with foster parents until married.

One child went to Texas, a bright and keen Italian boy, but very hard to manage. One, a Hebrew, grew to manhood and enlisted in the Navy.

(next page). Company of children for the New Sharon, Iowa distribution. In back, left to right: H. D. Clarke, Willie Mansfield, Willie Holman, Charles Kimmel, Willie Dicting. Middle row: George Heintz, Louis Zucco, Harry Dicting, Elizabeth Eagen, Samuel Thompson (Picelle), Ida Johnson, Blanche Heintz. Matilda Heintz is just above Johnson girl, but not very visible. The two little boys in the front are Ira Shongo and Thomas Zucco.

(top). Elizabeth Eagen.

(bottom). Left to right-Matilda, Blanche and George Heintz.

(top). William Holman.

(bottom). Ida Johnson.

Samuel Thompson (Picelle).

DUNLAP, IOWA - MARCH 4th, 1904

Children placed were:
Alta Barney, age 9 1/2, (taken by Mr. and Mrs. Van Slyke)
Edgar Barney, age 2, (taken by Mr. and Mrs. Solomon Gipson)
Elmer Barney, age 11, (taken by Mr. and Mrs. Solomon Gipson)
Ethel Barney, age 7, (taken by Risin and Elizabeth Malone)-(Author's
   note: Full names of Ethel's foster parents were obtained from Ethel's
   son, Robert Staley)
George Benson, age 7, (taken by Mr. and Mrs. Ora Malone)
Roscoe Benson, age 5, (taken by Mr. and Mrs. Ora Malone)
Michelena "Lena" Birraglio, age 13, (taken by Mrs. Sara Nelson)
Herman Cunna, age 9 1/2, (taken by Mr. and Mrs. A. N. Jordan)
Frank (or Willie?) Jones, age 6, (taken by Mr. and Mrs. Frank Bissell)
George Kemper, age 6, (taken by Mr. and Mrs. E. W. O'Banion)
Edward Melrose, age 3, (taken by Mr. and Mrs. George Cronkhite)
Edna Turner, age 7 1/2, (placed, then replaced five days later with Mr.
   and Mrs. John H. Anderson)
Henry Turner, age 6 1/2, (taken by Mr. and Mrs. Fred May)
Amanda Wallace, age 6 1/2, (taken by Mr. and Mrs. A. S. Lyman)
Lillian Wallace, age 3, (taken by Mr. and Mrs. C. M. Rife)

Some children placed later were:
Helen Hawks
Harry Henwood
Grace Turner-Gretman (placed with J. H. Anderson)
Florence Volkhart (placed later-see Mapleton, Iowa distribution)
George Volkhart (placed with W. A. Davie)
Annis Wells (placed with George Scott)
Mabel Wells (placed with Joseph Greenwood)

(Author's note: Information on the age of the children and who took
them was taken from the March 11th, 1904 edition of the *Dunlap
Reporter*, which ran a nice article on the distribution). The article read
as follows:

FIFTEEN ORPHAN CHILDREN FIND HOMES
WITH GOOD PEOPLE IN THIS VICINITY

A large crowd gathered at the Dunlap Opera House to inspect the children brought here under the direction of H. D. Clark for the purpose of finding new homes. Aside from the novelty of the occasion, there was a serious side. Many eyes filled with tears as the audience looked over the eager serious faces and watched the look of hope and disappointment that spread over the countenances of this little bunch of humanity.

Along with this came very affecting scenes, one little boy clinging to a brother a few years his senior and crying that he might not be taken from him. There were several applications for the older boy, but the little fellow stoutly refused to part with his baby brother and would not go with anyone unless he could take the baby. He gained the argument. Now it is hoped that both children and foster parents may grow together in love, for the good of both. As a general thing, the children are to be congratulated on securing such good homes. H. D. Clark sent a letter of appreciation to citizens of Dunlap.

On February 24th, 1904 I went to Albany, New York and got four children, which were brought to me by a County Superintendent. I took them back to New York City to become part of my party for the next distribution, which was at Dunlap, Iowa.

This was one of the best distributions I ever had and resulted in bringing many more there later on at different times. There were fifteen children in this distribution, which took place at the Opera House. All were placed except one boy, who had to be taken back to New York City with tonsillitis. All of these seemed to have a special history of much interest. A brother and sister from Nebraska were added to our company. I later had many single placings in Nebraska.

The Barney children were the ones I took from the County House near Albany. The girls were staying with their 78 year old grandmother and helped string buttons for a living. The father was George Barney, who was an engineer in a mill. Their mother was Eva C. Pullman. Ethel was born August 27th, 1896. She married and lived at Ute. Later on Edgar went to a widow lady who was a mother indeed. He married and farmed successfully. Elmer also turned out fine. He was born February 1st, 1893 at Coldbrook, New York. He was sent to the Boys' Lodging House, 44th Street, New York City. He married Marie M. Broderson of Denison, Iowa. Alta was born September 18th, 1894. She had a varied experience. Her foster mother was jealous of her and while the man was good to her and thought as much of her as a father could. In view of the jealousy, I had to take her away. I took her to Brooklyn, Iowa October 19th, 1908 and there she had great difficulties. She became headstrong and went out for herself and freedom, to which I consented. The experiences taught her lessons. At last, she settled down to farm work with a widow lady near West Liberty, Iowa and married Fred Howard of Tipton, Iowa in 1914. She now has three children. The others were legally adopted.

The Benson boys were very pretty boys, but had several replacings.

Michalena Birraglio was born in Italy May 8th, 1890. Her father had died and her mother married again to a Mr. Moore. Worthless. She had two or three homes in New York and was temporarily in the Orphan Asylum at Utica, New York. She was a most splendid girl of sixteen when I placed her with a widow, Mrs. Sarah Nelson. There were farmers in the family. She took the name Lena Nelson. In a few years her mother and a half brother found where she was and went to get her, but she would not leave. Her mother once came (along with a little brother) and offered her two hundred dollars if she would go with her, but she positively refused to leave Mrs. Nelson, who she later called "Grandma." She became an expert in blooded poultry and cattle and her foster mother gave her some stock and poultry with which she saved money. She bought Liberty bonds and put money in the Dunlap bank. She finally married Albert Nelson, her foster brother, on August 18th, 1923. I last visited them on November 14th and 15th, 1911. Lena died in childbirth at St. Anthony's Hospital, Carroll, Iowa on November 22nd, 1924. Their son is a pretty, healthy lad now and I hear occasionally from Mr. Nelson. He worships the boy and he did the mother Lena. My correspondence with Lena and the family and my visits there were easily the most pleasant of all I ever get from the wards. They raised many goats, as well as other stock.

I received a letter from her on January 3rd, 1915 that reads in part:

"I am ashamed for not answering your letter, it was neglect on my part, for Mr. Clarke, I think lots of you and I am sure I like to hear from you and would like to have you come and see us. Yes, I have almost forgotten my name. Once in a while we get thinking about it and try to spell it. It goes this way . . . M. M. B. - is that right? We are going to have a box supper to raise money for the minister. Will have a program with that . . . We have two hundred and fifty chickens, ninety-nine head of cattle, one hundred fifty pigs, and between fifteen and twenty cats! Plus six of the human race! Isn't that some family? We still have the auto and the invitation is still open for you . . . Now you will write to me. L.N."

Helen Hawks came later from Nebraska where she lost her long home of about thirteen years from deceit and theft, but after I took her away and talked so kindly to her about it, she never repeated the offenses and was a trustworthy girl.

Harry Henwood was robbed of schooling as the man was bound to make a hired man out of him without pay and being rather impudent about it. I took the boy away to another town where he should have schooling. George Volkhart came later and was with one of the members of the Iowa legislature and very domineering and insulting to me, but the boy also being stubborn, I let him stay.

Edna Turner was born June 15th, 1896 in New York City. Her father was Henry, an English Protestant. Her mother was Catherine McLoy, Canadian and deceased. Edna first came West with the Louisville, Nebraska Company of December 11th, 1903 and placed with her brother Henry at Springfield, Nebraska. Edna was a handsome girl and placed with a farmer in Dunlap, who took out adoption papers and I supposed he recorded them, but at her marriage he told her she was not adopted. That was a great shock to her. Her little brother was placed a few miles away. He was a pretty boy. Edna married well and happily to Guy Hanson on July 8th, 1914 and has three children. Her husband was for some time a druggist at Luverne,

Minnesota where I visited them on May 11th, 1915. They were so happy and contented. At this writing and for a long time, they have been in Sioux City, Iowa. She writes how happy she is and often sends a picture of the children and themselves.

On October 11th, 1914 I received a letter from her:

"Dear Mr. Clarke . . . you know when one gets married all we think of is how are we going to furnish and fix our home. We are now settled in our little home in Luverne, so we are in the same state you are. My! How I do wish you could come and see us. We both are happy. My husband works in the drug store. I with him Sunday afternoons and evenings. It makes it so nice for us and I do not have to stay at home all alone. Sunday is such a lonesome day. My husband is named G - . He is a blond and very nice looking. We had our pictures taken last week and will send you one. I surely did write to you about our love affairs, a nice long letter a couple of months before we were married. I am sorry you did not receive it. I wanted you to know all about me and I think of you every day and how kind you have been to us all . . . As ever, Edna."

Her sister Grace was in an orphanage hospital in Wartburg, New York with a bad case of eczema. They would not let her out for me to take until sixteen years of age. I then took her to Dunlap in November 1910 (meeting her at Chicago) to visit her sister Edna. It was a strange meeting, as they hardly seemed to know each other as sisters, but they soon became interested and were very happy together. Grace was very grateful for this and often wrote lovingly about it. She married at last in South Dakota, had a pretty child, but was separated from her husband, who seemed unworthy of her. She is at this writing (1928) in Kansas City, Missouri and has one girl named Geraldine.

Amanda and Lillian Wallace were sisters that were placed near each other, but were soon widely separated. Amanda was born July 22nd, 1897. She was replaced February 6th, 1907 with C. D. Travis of Carson, Iowa and called "Blanche Travis." I had photos taken of them before they were parted. Amanda died August 16th, 1911 and it was a pitiful letter the foster mother wrote of her loss and loneliness, though she had several children of her own. Lillian was born December 17th,

1900. She was called "Lelah Rife" at her new home. She was married to Alfred Peterson of Avoca, Iowa. I lost track of her in a few years.

Mabel Wells was born June 13th, 1894. She finally became a nurse in Independence, Missouri and was a very nice Christian girl. Annis, her sister, was born in 1899. She was placed in a fine home, but the family was moving to Seattle, Washington. She was seven years old at the time. Not being willing to adopt her, I did not let her go with them so far away. After they were settled in Seattle, they wrote they would adopt her and begged she be sent to them. I arranged for that and buying her a nice little hand bag, I gave her a pocket book and one dollar and twenty-five cents in dimes and nickels, a doll, pencil and paper and other toys. I bought a Pullman ticket for a four day trip, telegraphed them that I had started her on the journey and told the conductor she was worth her weight in diamonds. I had secured a berth for her in a Tourist Sleeper. Kissing her goodbye, I sent her off, never to see her again. She had only one change of cars to make between Dunlap, Iowa and Seattle and arrived safely. This occurred in May of 1906. She was met at the station by her new parents, Mr. and Mrs. George Scott, who telegraphed to say that she had more when she arrived than when she started. She and they often wrote to me. She became a beautiful girl, judged by her photo, and when sixteen years of age, while having her tonsils removed, bled to death on May 22nd, 1916. It was a sad home after that in Seattle and a sad day for me as well.

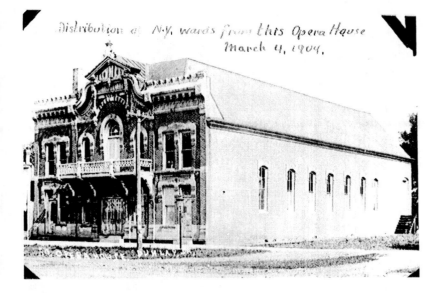

Distribution of N.Y. wards from this Opera House
March 4, 1904.

A view of the Opera House from which the Dunlap, Iowa distribution took place on March 4, 1904.

(top). Edgar Barney and his
foster mother.

(bottom). Elmer and Alta Barney.

128

(top left). Michelena Birraglio.

(top right). Helen Hawks, back right.

(bottom). Edna Turner with foster brothers.

Grace Turner.

Amanda (r) and Lillian Wallace (l).

MANILLA, IOWA - APRIL 15th, 1904

Some children placed were:
Charles Apgar (placed with Mark Simpson)
Harry Apgar
Mary Barrett
Rosa Barrett
Rose Mabel Barrtee
Reva Brewster (placed with Dell Plank of Dodge Center, Minnesota)
Alfred Brooks (placed with William and Cora Holmes at Earling,
  Iowa)
William Joseph Brooks (placed with A. R. Tryon at Defiance, Iowa)
Anna Davie (placed with Frank Brown)
Fred Gee
Samuel John Geleta
Harry Henwood
Clarendon Lindsley (placed with Dr. J. B. Gardner)
Marian Palmer
Mary Scallons
Nellie Scott (placed with Mrs. William Christie of Denison, Iowa)
Cornelia Smith
Howard Therein
Oliver Therein
Homer Thomas (placed with William Miller, then Carston Christensen
  of Denison, Iowa)
Horace Thomas
Cora Webb "Vera Beckman" (placed with Mrs. L. Beckman)
Annis Wells (see Dunlap, Iowa distribution)
Mabel Wells (see Dunlap, Iowa distribution)

On the twentieth of March, my wife and I started for New York City, visiting relatives on the way. On April sixth I went to Rochester, New York after two wards to take with me back to New York City. I stopped overnight at my brother-in-laws (Stephen Jennings) in Utica, NY and while I was there I went to the State Asylum and told the Matron and Secretary that I wanted a little girl to take to a friend in Minnesota, as I was to take a company of children from New York City in a few days to the west to place in homes. She brought before me five girls and told me to take my choice. I knew I could place all the girls and that they needed homes and so I said, "I'll take them all." We then took these children to New York City and added them to the others, who were selected for me by the Society.

On the twelfth of April, with Miss Anna Laura Hill as nurse and helper, along with my wife, we started for Manilla, Iowa. With seventeen children, passing enroute through Hormel, New York at midnight, a Salvation Army Captain approached us at the station and brought two sisters on board for us to take along. They said they had Indian blood in them. The parents of these two girls were vicious and degraded and yet they were beautiful girls and had a very pleasant disposition, although they were destined to trouble in the future.

Arriving at Chicago, the two boys I got at Rochester were met by their father and by previous arrangement, taken away by him. Later on when I visited them I found them in a home of squalor and poverty. A mother seemingly dying or already dead, as far as I could see, but they were the father's and that was the end of that. In transferring to the buses in Chicago, three girls were missing. The crowd had swept them away from us. The first instance of the kind I had ever known. My wife followed them up on Dearborn Street and got two of them while she carried a baby in her arms. The third was nowhere to be seen. Taking them back to the bus, I wandered about many blocks trying to find her, but of no avail. We then went over to the C.M. & St. Paul station and there I telephoned to the second police precinct, which was near the Dearborn station and I said to the Chief, "In coming through Chicago with a company of orphan children to take west for homes, I lost near the Dearborn station, a little girl named Cornelia Smith. She is eight years old and has black hair, black eyes and a dark complexion. She is a little pale from sickness because of riding on the train. She wore a tamoshanter cap, blue coat trimmed with braid, a red checked dress and carried a bundle." I suppose that was phoned to all the police stations in the city and in three hours I got a phone call saying they had found her. I replied that I would come after her and the police said, "No, we'll bring her to you." She came in a patrol wagon with two burley policeman and was put into my arms. She had wandered three miles away and was found in a drug store. I surely kissed that child in my joy at finding her. She said she was not scared, but thought all the time that she was following me! Five years later, I took this girl back to New York to the hospital, having been taken strangely sick. Her name was changed to Doty Ivey. The local doctor said he could not help her and she said to her foster mother, "Send for Mr. Clarke, he will help me." She was then thirteen years of age, could not walk and I took her in my arms (along with my satchel) to the train. I "mothered" her all the way to New York City. I had a Pullman section. Not a woman on our car spoke to her on the journey, though they knew I was caring for her. One lady in a rear car came in and braided her hair and tied the ribbons, but I had to do it all over again, it was such a poor job. At Jersey City I secured a wheel chair and wheeled her to the ferry and then secured a taxi and thence went to the hospital. In three weeks she was convalescent. In the meantime I found her sister in New Jersey to whom she went for a visit. Later, I took her back to her Manilla, Iowa home. When she became of age, she went under protest of foster parents to this sister who had married, and was soon turned away. In her mental condition, she was soon taken to the Asylum at Rome, New York. She died there at about age nineteen.

Charles Apgar was born in April of 1895 at Hornellsville, New York. His father was crippled. Charles was received from the Superintendent of the Poor at Binghamton, New York. He later moved to Wayne, Nebraska and served in the World War. Harry Apgar was in the World War.

The two Barrett sisters from Hornell were placed near each other. The elder was replaced in several homes. Mary was born May 21st, 1891. She claims she is part Indian. She would steal and falsify. She stole a watch in a house where the owner was in the same room and did not observe it. She confessed to it two weeks later. She made much trouble in Des Moines, Iowa and we had to protect her in Court and have the appointment of a guardian annulled, who was appointed because of her confessed falsehoods. She had told things against the foster parents and the woman agent of the Humane Society, without any investigation, permitted publication of the stuff. She said that I had placed her in a restaurant and abandoned her and she was being robbed of sufficient clothes and schooling. At last, she ran away and married a miserable drunkard.

Rosa Barrett was born July 11th, 1893. She was quite a good girl. She stayed in her home until a few days before turning of age and then eloped with a man old enough to be her father, but repented and asked my forgiveness and later married happily to Lonnie L. Lotz of Winfield, Iowa and writes me good letters of appreciation of her home I placed her in and of my kindness and help. She was at work in Omaha the last I knew.Their father was M. L. Barrett, a Woodman, born at Putney, Yates County, New York. Their mother was Hannah Conkling of Almond, New York. They were surrendered by the father at Cameron, New York on March 28th, 1904. Ensign Urban of the Salvation Army brought the two sisters to the train at Hornell, New York when I was passing through.

Little Reva Brewster was born April 14th, 1900 in Elmira, New York. I brought her from the New York Orphan Asylum at Utica. Reva was reserved for the Dodge Center home of Dell Plank that I had promised. She was adopted in 1905. She grew up, graduated from High School and married R. J. Reider in Luck, Wisconsin, from where she occasionally writes.

Alfred Brooks was born November 28th, 1902.William Joseph Brooks was born October 3rd, 1899.

Anna Davie was born April 28th, 1899. She was taken by the Mayor of the town. She graduated at High School and was a fine pianist.

Fred Gee was born November 4th, 1894. He had several homes and was then returned to his mother and relatives at Dansville, New York. I visited him there in December 1924.

The other baby was an Austrian named Samuel Geleta. He was born October 14th, 1902. He was a beautiful child and had varied experience. He was replaced July 22, 1908. I lost all track of him in a few years, but in five years after placing, I took him back to a New York Hospital (February 10th, 1909) to save his foot that had been injured. I visited him there July 3rd, 1909. He then went to other homes and is now in Cameron, New York.

Arriving at Manilla, I called J. B. Gardner, a doctor, to see Cornelia Smith, and while he was busy with her, the baby on the floor crawled to him. He went home and told his wife that there was a baby for her to take and the next morning at the Opera House, the doctor and wife took little Clarendon Lindsley. He was born October 20th, 1902. He was later called "Ray Gardner." He had good care and was loved, but he died on October 21st, 1912, greatly to their grief.

Marion Palmer was born November 3rd, 1893 in Connecticut. Her parents were George and Annie of CosCob, Connecticut. They were American Protestants. Her mother had died and Marian was received by the Five Points House of Industry in New York and from the Society for the Prevention of Cruelty to Children on August 19th, 1902. She was transferred to the Children's Aid Society on April 11th, 1904. She was a very affectionate girl and several years after being placed, would come to see my wife and I and stay a week. Enroute to Manilla, I left her in care of a friend at Marion, Iowa on April 14th, 1904, until I came back and placed her. She was placed in Wadena, Iowa with Mr. and Mrs. C. B. Phillips. Various complaints were made by neighbors that she was abused and in danger and all that. Investigation revealed no harm, but I replaced her in Hayfield, Minnesota with Mr. and Mrs. Clarence McPeek, not far from my own home. She became very much attached to us and came every year to make us a visit. Then she wrote me of various freaks. Finally, I received anonymous letters purporting to be from some neighbor who would witness the abuse of the girl. When investigated, it was found to be untrue. The girl would deny it all. She seemed very happy. Her foster parents indulged her in many pleasures and visits where she could go safely. Though there were no youthful companionships nearby, and all were of different nationalities. Marion was superior to these in school and that seemed to make jealousies.

On one of her visits to us she was particularly happy. After she returned home we discovered a breast pin gone that I had bought for my wife in Des Moines once and sent her for her birthday. We never knew she had stolen anything in her life. I went to visit her purposely to find out. I said nothing to her about the pin, but when she went up stairs I asked her foster mother if she had a new pin. She said she had. I asked to see it. She went up stairs to get it and the girl at once became suspicious and would not come down again until sent for. Her foster mother thought it was some cheap affair she had bought somewhere. The girl came down crying and I forgave her with all my heart. I told her to come and see us all the same, which she did and nothing more was said about it. They moved to another town and the girl then wanted to go to Connecticut to see her own father, which she did and he met her at the station drunk. I had told her he and her brother were drunkards and tried to keep her from going. She soon returned. Her actions were strange and she seemed to love her foster father intensely and different from daughter and father. The family in disgust took her to the insane asylum, but friends quickly got her out. After that she worked out and married in Iowa. I found on comparing the anonymous letters referred to with her own handwriting, that they were the same. She had no doubt written them herself for adventure. I had a report in 1915 that her husband, Andrus Johnson, had her taken to an insane asylum. They had two children. A few such cases as this would make good study in Eugenics and Euthenics. She was a very industrious and capable girl. Was this mostly environment or heredity?

Mary Scollons was placed while enroute to Manilla and when of age, went to work for a widow at Strawberry Point, Iowa. She later died and the lady paid all her funeral expenses. She was a dear Christian Irish girl.

Nellie Scott was born March 31st, 1892 at Brooklyn, New York. She came from the House of Refuge. Her father Frank was an American Protestant and her mother was an English Protestant. She has a brother Herbert in Maryland. She was taken at Denison and was a sad girl. She married her foster brother, a Christie, and they have children.

Homer Thomas was born October 1898 in Sweden. He and his brother Horace were surrendered by their father on November 28th, 1903. Their mother was Ada Martin.

Cora Webb was born May 4th, 1895 at Trenton, New York. She had several sisters. Her father was Thomas was born in England

and was a Protestant laborer. Her mother's name was Emma, also an English Protestant. Cora was surrendered to the Society for the Prevention of Cruelty to Children, and was then committed to the New York Orphan Asylum at Utica on January 3rd, 1901. She was called "Vera Beckman" in Manilla. She was taken by a merchant and ruined by his clerk. The clerk was the son of a wealthy physician and was arrested, but Iowa law released a man who ruined a girl over fifteen years of age. Her foster sister and husband took her to Sturgis, South Dakota, far out on a ranch. Her foster father died and her foster sister cared for her and educated her well in music. She later went back to Manilla and was sent to a Convent by Protestants!! She was later sent to her mother, a ruined girl. I had found her sisters by accident in New York State. Arriving at her sister's (Mrs. John Lyman, Coldbrook, New York), she stayed only three days and then went to destruction as far as could be learned. It was a very pitiful case and we fought hard for her rescue. The question is, where is the blame to be attached?

Not exactly in this connection, but suggested by our visits between the distributions of wards who seem to be making good, I will mention one Frances Dennis, a little black-eyed brunette, occasionally visited. Sometimes I found her at the school house for a few minutes and what was said had to be fast between trains. She was born May 31st, 1888 and placed at Audubon, Nebraska. She has a brother Don in Audubon. She was quick, alert, serious and frivolous at the same time. She enjoyed a bit of praise, which she seemed to never forget. Later, her people moved to the Pacific coast and few were the letters received for some time. Her foster father died and after staying with the widowed foster mother until about nineteen years of age, she received about fifty dollars and earned enough more working out to attend a Business College. Soon she became a traveling companion and secretary of an authoress all over the country and Mexico. The authoress (I have a little booklet of her poems) was failing in health. Frances again went for herself in some bookkeeping I think. Her letters became exceedingly interesting. Soon she was engaged to marry whom she supposed to be a worthy and fine young man and whose parents greatly encouraged the "match." Just a few days before the wedding was to take place, she discovered that the said "splendid young man" had children in different parts of the state and was wholly unworthy of her. This nearly "broke her up." Faith in humanity was almost gone. She wrote about it and I told her to hold her head up and be so thankful that she escaped the sure troubles she would have had had she married him.

Continuing her work faithfully and acting on my advice, she later on married happily to all reports.

Extracts from some of her letters:

"January 8th, 1911 -
Dear Friend,

Your welcome letter was received at San Jose and appreciated very much . . . I sent you a book of poems as a gift for Xmas. Did you receive it? Santa was very good to me this year and I received many books, a beautiful sweater, cards, etc. I am taking a post-graduating course in bookkeeping. Expect to take more when this is finished. I may have a good education by the time I am old! I'll forget all I learned at one school before I take another, since I graduated at High School. Can't realize the fact of my age when a few years ago I was in the Home. Well, Mr. Clarke, I often wonder that I am as good a girl I am and didn't go to ruin. Mrs. D. not being a Christian and nagging and scolding constantly, and no love for me at all, no companions, . . . I just felt I did not care what became of me, but I overcame that and came out victorious at last. As to marriage, I don't know. I have not an over stock of love for men. Marriage is for life . . . I loved once and lost. He would do things like card playing and dancing and would not leave them for me. He got them and lost me. What a man will not do for his sweetheart, he will not do for his wife. Down in my heart this is just killing me. I loved him and do yet, but I try to be jolly and overcome it, and I will . . . I have about six hundred postals received from friends all over the world. I want a photo of you to add to my collection of photos. Wishing you a happy, prosperous new year. I am Frances D."

Again, on January 27th:

" Dear Mr. Clarke, . . . certainly glad to hear from you. I am still in Business College and hope to be capable of the best positions and a good salary. I hope you will have one girl that you will be

proud of, a Christian above all. I do not care to know anything about my history. What you don't know never hurts you. My brother was married and he called on me for some money! It's a shame if he can't support a wife he ought not to have married . . . No, I'll get my own living and no one's else . . . Work is very dull here now, especially for book keepers and Stenographers. I never was out of work and I am helping a friend until I can get another position at not less than fifteen dollars per week...I am glad you are proud of me and hope you always will be . . . "

Again, on November twelfth:

"I will whisper a little secret to you. I am going to be married this winter some time. The unfortunate young gentleman is a promising Pacific Electrician. He is not a beauty and he is not one of the 'smart-licky' kind, but he is good and won me by his goodness. I am going to forget the past and make a success and have the education to make a successful home. I certainly look to you as a father more than as to a friend and I want your blessing . . . I visit the County Hospital every Sunday and take the poor people something . . . Write me a long letter. Frances. " Such letters prove that many girls and boys are not failures.

It would seem that an unusual number of unhappy endings came to this fine group of children, for in many respects we never had a more promising company than these we had for Manilla.

(top left). Charles Apgar in 1912.

(top right). Rosa Barrett.

(bottom). Reva Brewster.

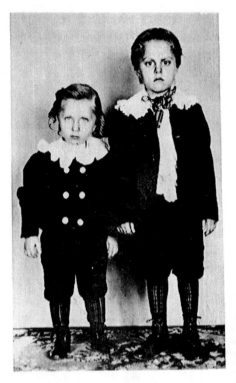

(top). William (r) and Alfred
Brooks (l).

(bottom). Annie Davie.

(top). Samuel John Galeta.

(bottom). Fred Gee.

Clarendon Lindsley.

(top). Marian Palmer.

(bottom). Nellie Scott.

(top). Homer Thomas.

(bottom). Cora Webb.

Annis (l) and Mabel Wells (r).

MAPLETON AND COON RAPIDS, IOWA - JUNE 16TH, 1904

<u>Some children placed in Mapleton were</u>:
Bessie Beach (left at Marion, Iowa)
Annie Jane Dailey
Dorothy Dailey (placed with Mrs. Clara McLaughlin)
Luella Maude Davenport (placed later with Walter and Sadie Barker of York, Nebraska)
Amelia Fredericks (left at Marion, Iowa-later placed with Mrs. John Buckley of Byron, Minnesota)
Valentine O'Day (placed with Mrs. Mary Johnson)
Nellie Scott (see Manilla, Iowa distribution)
Ethel "Helen" Skogland (left at Marion, Iowa)
Florence Volkhart
Anna Wood

<u>Some children placed in Coon Rapids were</u>:
Charles Gartland
James McCann (placed with James Dailey)
Martha McCann (placed with Charles Patrick and called "Louise Patrick")
Sadie McCann
Bertha Schmidt (replaced later with Willard Van Horn of Garwin, Iowa)
Ernest Schmidt (replaced in Missouri in 1905 and with J. P. Stotler in West Branch, Iowa in 1908)
George Smith (placed with T. M. Campbell)
John J. Smith
Julius Smith (placed with A. C. Taylor)
Maud Smith (placed with A. C. Taylor, as above)

These two distributions were on the same day. I had previously arranged for them. B. W. Tice and myself, associated together, had made these. We had came out together and then parted at Coon Rapids, where he was to place half of them, and I went on to Mapleton. Having over thirty children, it was necessary to have more than one nurse or lady with us. I telegraphed my daughter Mabel at Alfred Station, New York to meet us in Buffalo, New York at about midnight and join us. We had Miss Hill along to assist Mr. Tice and I had my wife and daughter to assist me.

On the way out I left Bessie Beach with her applicant at Marion, Iowa, who took her at the train and went on to Oelwein, Iowa. He was a merchant and soon took a baby from another home and turned off Bessie. She was born June 5th, 1898. She was one of the handsomest girls I had placed. She was lively and winsome with curly black hair. Her grief was great as she had to leave her home, but more than that, the baby she had begun to love that they had taken. She began to cry as we went enroute to her new home, saying we had gone more than ten miles (we had gone over forty). She said, "If I don't have to go more than ten miles I can sometimes go to see the baby." She never saw that baby again. After placings in three or four homes and much sadness for her, at last she married October 1st, 1914 to Charles C. Tallman "for a home," unhappily. This was at Clarion, Iowa. Her little girl, Audrea, is her great comfort.

On May 1st, 1914 she wrote this letter to me:

"You don't know how glad I was to receive your letter. It seemed like getting back a good old friend. So you went back to New York. You must tell me all about it. Then you must give me my history. I can hardly wait for it. You don't know how I want to see you. When you settle may be I'll come and see you. If I ever get into trouble of any kind, you will be the one I shall ask to help me. I'd be afraid to trust anyone else."

On May eighteenth she writes again:

"You don't know how glad I was to hear from you and have my questions answered. Of course, it was not as much as I wanted to know. You said the Society for the Prevention of Cruelty to Children took me away from my parents. What for? Were they mean to me? It must have been for some such reason. Were they willing for me to go? Did you ever see them? What kind of people were they? Do you know for sure my name? Names are sometimes changed and I wondered if such was my case. You'll tell me won't you Mr. Clarke? You can't blame a girl for wanting to know if her parents are alive. If

I were ashamed of them I'd like to see them. I wonder if they ever think of me? They were no doubt poor people were they not? You don't know how my heart craves to know the whole truth. It seems like I'll never be happy 'til I know. Were my parents in New York when I was taken away? Forgive me if you think I am bold . . . you are a father to me. I'm not afraid to ask you anything. When I get married you just come and stay a whole month with me. Ha, ha."

Again she wrote on September twenty-first:

"Forgetting you would be impossible after knowing you so long and you being so good to me and watching over me so long ever since I was a baby. I have news for you. I'm to be married a week from next Thursday. He is a Presbyterian . . . twenty-two years old. We will go to housekeeping in a week or so. He asked me about my parents and I told him they were dead. Let it go at that . . . Love at first sight! You are welcome to my home any time. Seems funny that I am to be married. Better be in school. I guess it is all right. Write to me right away. Lovingly. Bessie."

These are sample letters of inquiry about parents and the great anxiety to know when they are grown up.

In this Mapleton company were two Irish sisters, one not very strong mentally and after being replaced three or four times, she was sent back to New York. Her name was Annie Jane Dailey. Had I been able to get to her, I could have prevented that, as I certainly should under all the circumstances. She had such confidence in me and appealed to me so earnestly. The roads were so impassable I could not reach the place and she was sent. The other sister fell into the hands of a wealthy family who moved later to Denver, Colorado. Dorothy Dailey was born January 12th, 1895.

On September 7th, 1914 she wrote:

"My Dear Friend,

I have been back east (Iowa) on a visit. I had a lovely time, visiting my old friends at Mapleton. Also visited in other cities and towns. Started in school last Monday. Today is Labor Day and vacation. You have never told me anything about myself. I think that I am now old enough to know. I suppose it is written in the books somewhere. I would be very thankful to you if you could tell me all you can. It seems awful to go through this world not knowing more about myself than I do. There are important questions I can not answer because I know so little. Please write and tell me about these things. Billy Sunday is here and we are praying that many Denver people will be saved. The tabernacle was crowded yesterday. Hoping you will be able to give the information asked, I am . . . D. D."

It seems later she became too proud to know about her sister or write to her. Later still, she ceased all interest with me.

After placing the children at Mapleton, I left my wife and daughter to get a livery and make the first visits to the respective homes of the wards. I took the baby, Luella Maud Davenport, age about thirteen months, and headed to York, Nebraska. I was a night and a day making the trip and was all alone with the baby. She was good all the way. She was born May 4th, 1903. Maudie became a most interesting child. I had not seen her in five years when I went to visit her at her foster home, where she was later legally adopted. She was dressed for the occasion and waiting for me, just as though she had known me all these years. She had infantile paralysis and had to drag one limb as she came to me. Later, she recovered from this. All the day long, we had a happy visit and when I came away, she cried after me.

On June 20th, 1914 I received this letter from her:

"Dear Friend,

It is ten years today that you brought me here and I want to thank you very much for giving me a good home . . . We had Children's Day Service and I sang a solo and spoke. All the people thought I did very well . . . I would like to see you. I have twelve little chickens, fifteen pigs, twelve calves, six little geese and three old hens. Good by. Write soon."

She later graduated at the Music Conservatory and married J. Allen Beattie on January 22nd, 1926. She had brothers Amos and Lawrence in the French War and a sister, Mrs. Vath, of Fort Dodge, Iowa. She now lives at York, Nebraska.

Amelia Fredericks (German) I had also left with friends at Marion as I passed through. I placed her later in Minnesota on June 27th, 1904. A fine home. She was born January 22, 1893. Almost annually she would come to see Mrs. Clarke and myself, beside my annual visits. When some past seventeen she wanted to marry a young man and I discouraged her. Later, she left her home to work out and then asked again to marry him. Mrs. Clarke and I made her a wedding at our home and the parents of the young man, not yet of age, came and gave consent, or had to! She was married to Elmer Christopherson of Kasson, Minnesota on June 19th, 1911. In four months he deserted her and went to Wisconsin. In two years I went with her to Winona, Minnesota and assisted her in getting a divorce. Very soon after that he returned, promising to do better, and they again went to living together. After having two children, a boy and girl, he ran away again. I took her to her father-in-laws. Hungry for his baby, he again came back, but he had lost his job and was destitute. She came to me for help and I took her to my house. She went back and forth to her former foster mother, who later died. Again they went to house keeping. Still later on she deserted him and HE was in deepest grief! I succeeded in restoring them and at last account (1922) they were again living happily, having both had a bitter experience. They now live at LaCrosse, Wisconsin.

In the same lot of children was a baby of two years, Charles Gartland, whose father was in Sing Sing prison and whose mother was addicted to drink. His father was a Protestant from Florida. His mother's name was Lizzie Bannin, a Catholic. A charitable woman of "Do-Ye-Next-Thing Society" came with her to surrender the child. I took the babe up in my arms and he put his tiny hands on my neck and said, "Papa." He too, is still in his farm home.

James McCann was born March 7th, 1898 and was placed in Letcher, South Dakota on June 16, 1904. I visited him April 12th, 1911. Martha McCann was born November 3rd, 1893. She later went by "Louise Patrick." Sadie McCann was born in 1901. She is married to Walter King in Nebraska now. Their parents names were Julia and John, Irish Protestants that were separated. The children were placed in the House of Industry, Five Points, New York on March 25th, 1901. Three of their children died. Two other sisters are named Annie and Mamie. The above children were taken from the Society for the Prevention of Cruelty to Children to the Refuge.

Valentine O'Day was born March 27th, 1898.

Ethel Skogland (sister of Agnes at Corydon, Iowa) was also left at Marion, but later was taken to Humeston, Iowa. She was born May 24th, 1896. She was legally adopted in 1912 as "Helen Palmer." She went to her sister Agnes at San Jon, New Mexico and then back to Humeston. She married Harry Biggs of Galesburg, Illinois. She was a bright affectionate girl and did well.

Anna Wood was the most tragic of any life of this company. She was placed with a baker and his wife, but stayed but two or three days when she was taken by a farmer in a neighboring town. In that home a foster sister has clung to her all these years with yearning. Nellie Baker was her name and she continued to be Anna's best friend for years, settling in Idaho and becoming a teacher. Anna had to be replaced several times and finally went back to New York City and after a year or two in many places, was sent to the Newark Custodial Asylum to stay until about forty-five years of age, if she lives that long. She had a little money that I had placed in a bank for her, where it remained for six years, as I had lost track of her. Then I found where she was and used the money for her benefit. She is a very sad girl there, often begging me to get her out if possible, but I have no jurisdiction as I did not have her go there. I have visited her a few times when making trips east. She calls me "Daddy Clarke." The last two times were 1924 and 1926. I send her little presents and she says I am her only friend on earth except for Nellie Baker.

In this Mapleton company were two brothers that I took from a mother in the city who had came with them to the office saying that she had six children and was paying eleven dollars a month for a room to live in and could not support her children. She gave us the baby and the boy of four years. These have kept the homes I found them all these eleven years.

Passing by all the rest of the Mapleton party, I'll mention Florence Volkhart, who went to a widow out of town. Florence was born May 17th, 1893. She came West with her brother George in the Sidney, Iowa Company. They were surrendered by Theodore Walter, an uncle from Lakewood, New Jersey, on September 14th, 1905. Their father's name was George and their mother was Rosa Walter,

Protestants. Their stepfather was Thomas Harmon of New York City. The children were abandoned after the mother's death in May 1905. In a few years I helped her to attend a Seventh Day Adventist Academy at Stuart, Iowa and secured money for her expenses. She then worked out and went to Denison near where her brother George lived. I had last visited her in Des Moines. While there she became insane and poisoned herself and a baby of the family (Glasscock) and both died.

After Mr. Tice had placed the Coon Rapids company I had charge of them to visit and replace if necessary. In this company there were five Smiths and two Schmidts. Later I united an older sister to the Smiths who was overjoyed to meet and be near her kin.

Bertha Schmidt was born October 8th, 1895. She was first placed in Missouri in 1905 and then replaced in 1909. She was married in 1903 to George O'Connell of Newark, New York. She has a sister Clara, among others, and a brother Ernest. Ernest Schmidt was born March 18th, 1903. He was first placed in Missouri in 1905 and then replaced on December 11th, 1908 with J. P. Stotler of West Branch, Iowa. He later moved to Tipton, Iowa and attended Grinnell College. He entered West Point in New York as a Cadet in Company "B" U.S.M.A. in July 1923.

Julius Smith was born June 16th, 1900. Maud Smith was born March 17th, 1898. George Smith was born in 1893 or 1896. They have a half brother named John J. Smith, born in 1892, who was also placed in Coon Rapids. In addition, they have a half sister named Mabel Bonney.

In June of this year I received the following application from a little girl:
"Dear Mr. Clark,

I am a little girl and my name is Lottie Ehret. I am seven years old. and I am so lonely that I want a little brother and sister. I want sister older than brother. I want sister four years. I want brother two years old. I want them bright. and I will be good to them and I will make them happy. When can you get them for me. Please direct this letter to Lottie Ehret, Salem, West Virginia.

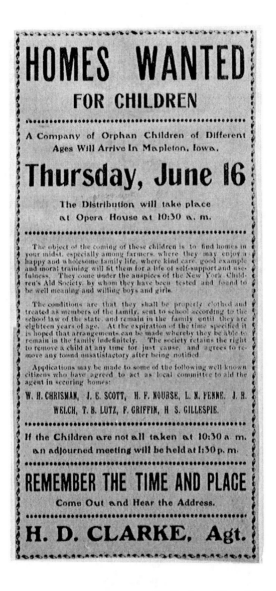

Dodger for the Mapleton, Iowa distribution of June 16, 1904.

Bessie Beach.

Dorothy Dailey.

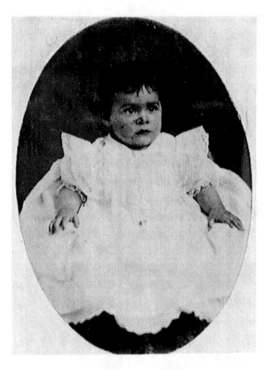

Luella Maude Davenport at age thirteen months in York, Nebraska.

Amelia Fredericks and husband.

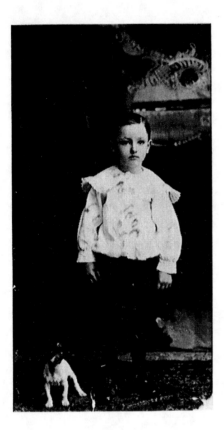

(top left). Charles Gartland.

(top right). Left to right: Martha, James and Sadie McCann.

(top). Martha and James McCann.

(bottom). Valentine O'Day.

161

(top). Bertha Schmidt (back right) with foster parents and their children.

(bottom). Ernest Schmidt.

Ethel "Helen" Skogland.

Agnes Skogland.

Left to right: Maude, George and Julius Smith.

John J. Smith.

GRISWOLD, IOWA - JULY 22nd, 1904

Some children placed were:
Leon Abel
Charles Anderson
James Gordon Bennett
Jennie Dickenson (placed with J. P. Gardiner)
Maggie Dickenson (placed with L. M. Jackson and replaced with T. S. Ellis)
Nellie Dickenson (placed with T. S. Ellis, as above)
Jacob Fendel (placed with Henry Steinbeck)
Paulina Harrison (placed with M. C. Goudie)
John Johnson (placed with Cris Fisher of Grant, Iowa)
Boy-Johnson
Boy-Johnson (came later)
Blanch Kent (placed in Pacific Junction, Iowa)
Maud Kent (placed with Clarkson Godfrey and later with Mrs. Frank Kimberly of Collins, Iowa)
Harry McKenzie (see "Guardianships")

The methods of these distributions were about all of a sameness. The children however, were all of a different history and make up. Each one had some characteristics that were of interest and could be recorded with profit. I found that many families well recommended by the local committees were lacking in common sense and their dispositions were not suitable for bringing a child up well. Of course, all these were average families in many respects and had the children been their own, they would have had to keep them and probably spoil them.

Three Irish sisters named Dickenson were along. Their mother had died and the father was a drunk and they were in filth and rags. Jennie was born July 22nd, 1900. She was adopted at the first and well educated and when her foster father died she cared for her foster mother while she lived and did all affection could do for her comfort and happiness. She went to College and is the assistant of a lawyer as a stenographer and typist in Des Moines, Iowa. Maggie Dickenson was born July 20th, 1896. She became a nurse and did well. I visited them in Des Moines in October, 1925. Nellie Dickenson married Carl Jones after much trouble and a tragic time of it, and has several children living in poverty. They now live in Atlantic, Iowa. She was a very hard worker all her life and wherever she lived.

Jacob Fendel was born April 16th, 1897.

Paulina Harrison was born in 1889 or 1890. She was first placed in Falls City, Nebraska in December 1903 with C. S. Pearce. She was sent to Belle Plaine and Welton, Iowa and Milton, Wisconsin. She married W. L. Pearce in Nebraska and moved to Langdon, Missouri. They then moved to Boone, Iowa and now have two children.

John Johnson was born August 10th, 1892. He is now married and lives near Cumberland, Iowa.

In this company were two sisters, Blanch and Maud Kent, quite different in disposition. Blanch was utterly spoiled with supposed kindness, but which is not real kindness. The self reliance and appreciation of a child comes from having suitable work and restraint. Their father was George Kent, deceased and their mother was Mary Mardy, who left the children two and a half years without visiting. She was last heard from on December 16th, 1916. The children were placed in the Home for the Friendless in New York. Blanch was placed with a baggage master on the C. B. & Q. Railway. She was paid for all the little errands she did and was permitted to idle away her time and in many ways spoiled so that in time she had to lose her home, unfit for another. Maud Kent was born in Brooklyn, New York. She had several good homes. She was a very affectionate girl. She visited her sister in Pacific Junction, Iowa on August 3rd, 1906. Her last home that I secured with Mrs. Frank Kimberly of Collins, Iowa was one of wealth and beauty. They did all that money could do for her comfort and happiness, but she was always discontented. At last she came to me from Iowa into Minnesota with a large Saritoga trunk, well filled with nice clothes. I hired her out to a farmer at three dollars a week and she was happy. Her foster mother came to my house to meet her and seemed interested in her and made her frequent presents. At last she went back into Iowa, married Ralph Smith on September 13th,

1912 in Ankeny, Iowa, and had one girl. She divorced her husband and received a lot of money from him, but used it all up and was thrown upon the world at last, unprepared to meet its temptations, and she made shipwreck. I lost all track of her.

The boys of the company did fairly well. One of these was named after an illustrious journalist, but was far from having any journalistic abilities. He drifted about from home to home with various fortunes and with families with sense, and some with little of that needful quality. It was strange how some families with best of recommendations would turn out so completely devoid of common sense. Every trivial fault of a child was the occasion of some long letter fearful of results in taking him. This boy however was full of faults and yet some very good qualities. He was very affectionate, willing to work, though not very honest about it. He managed to stay several years with his last foster father. I visited him in 1915.

Jacob Fendel.

Nellie (l), Jennie (m) and Maggie Dickenson (r).

(top). Paulina Harrison.

(bottom). John Johnson at age nine.

(top). Blanche (l) and Maud (r) Kent.

(bottom). Harry McKenzie.

SIDNEY, IOWA - SEPTEMBER 22nd, 1904

<u>Some children placed were</u>:
Thomas Dailey
Margaret Hunt
Robert Hunt
Sarah Hunt
Henry Fleischmann
Freda Landers (twin)
Lizzie Landers (twin)
Paul Medler
Alice Quince (placed with James Easley)
Bella Quince (placed in twelve homes in three years)
Margaret Robins
Eva May Seaman (twin)-(replaced with Mrs. Lizzie Hegwood on
  December 9th)
Iva Ella Seaman (twin)
Lillian Vermilyea
Florence Volkhart (see Mapleton, Iowa distribution)
George Volkhart
Daniel Van Wicklen

We had an interesting company, but later events brought about very discouraging results. A few remained in homes and apparently did well. No doubt the rest would have turned out much better had their first homes been devoted to their best interests. This distribution took place from the Methodist Church at 10:00 a.m. and 2:00 p.m. The Five Points House of Industry in New York furnished many in this company.

The Landers twins were most beautiful girls. They were modest and wonderful songsters. How they could sing! They were simply angelic and created a profound sensation. A physician and wife in Nebraska took them and were so happy with them that the doctor sold out his practice and moved with them to another state where it would not be known that they were not his own children. They were kept from writing to any former friends, but could write to a brother in Nebraska.

Paul Medler had a brother Harry and a sister Viola placed from the Louisville, Nebraska distribution of December 11th, 1903.

Not to mention each one in particular, Alice Quince and sister were pretty girls and fine singers. Alice was born November 1, 1894. She was placed with the Misses Easley of the family of James Easley. She was often requested by the Baptist pastor to sing solos in church, which drew people who would not go simply to hear him preach. She was a fine Contralto singer. She was taken by an old couple, who had two unmarried and over-religious maids that so nagged the girl on virtue and religion that they seemed to make a little hypocrite of her. Alice was a beautiful girl. She married a fine man in Chappauqua, New York on November 15th, 1913, a soldier named C. V. Swanson, but then deserted him and her beautiful baby girl in October 1916 and went to live with a brother in Brooklyn. Her husband had written to me for six years and the little girl also sends little messages, calling me "Uncle Clarke" and "Grandpa Clarke."

Bella Quince was born October 11th, 1892. She was one who had more homes than any other ward I ever placed. Twelve homes in three years, besides several boarding places. She seemed to quickly understand that if she lost a home, I'd quickly get her another. I asked the Society to send for her to come back and they said, "Clothe her, board her, anything but sending her back." She had already had a record. So I kept her going. She accused almost every home where she was placed as immodest. She was bold and defiant, but very nice in many ways. She was a very winning girl. Her history was too long and tragic to detail. When she was fifteen years of age I sent her back to New York by the nurse, Miss Hill. On October 16th, 1907 they put her in the Reform School (Elizabeth Home) for a year and then placed her out until age eighteen, when she and her foster mother begged me to get her a position in Iowa so she could be in the same state with her sister Alice. I got her a clerkship in a store, but she only kept it a few weeks. She fell in love with all the young men who traded with her. In spite of my admonition not to go to her sister until her sister was of age, she went and made such a row that Alice was sent back to New

York in 1912 and came to grief. Bella continued her course until at last she was ruined and married, though I never saw her after she was fifteen. She ran away with a show troop and became a mother. I helped her many times. She ended up in Leavenworth, Kansas. She and Alice were said to have a sister Mamie and a brother William.

Margaret Robins was a nice girl, went to Nebraska and finally back to friends in the east.

The Seaman twins had to be separated. Iva Ella returned to New York and Eva May stayed on a farm in Lenox, Iowa. Eva May was born July 9th, 1895.

Lillian Vermilyea was understood to come from the aristocracy. She looked it. Had a very stubborn will, but was a good girl. She was born June 2nd or 27th, 1891.

There were two sisters and a brother in the company, the oldest of which gave me great trouble and her two foster parents or homes were downright ugly to me at times. At last I secured her a home where she got a High School education and then she went back, breaking her promise and was at last accounts bitter in feeling.

One of the boys in this company was a pet and of keenest and loveliest disposition. He, with a few others, could not be placed at Sidney, so I took them to other towns.

In some respects it was a most remarkable company that landed at Sidney. We had thirty-five applications for them. The local papers had a great write-up of the occasion.

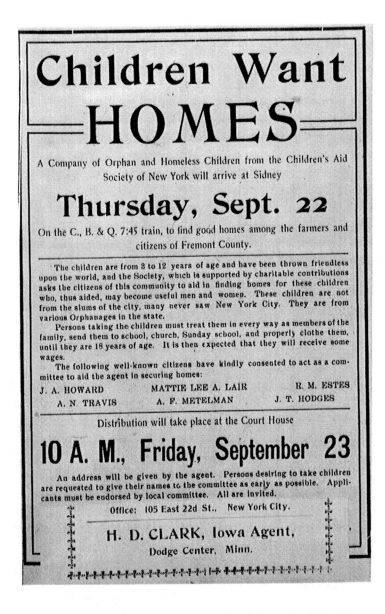

Children Want
—HOMES—

A Company of Orphan and Homeless Children from the Children's Aid Society of New York will arrive at Sidney

Thursday, Sept. 22

On the C., B. & Q. 7:45 train, to find good homes among the farmers and citizens of Fremont County.

The children are from 8 to 12 years of age and have been thrown friendless upon the world, and the Society, which is supported by charitable contributions asks the citizens of this community to aid in finding homes for these children who, thus aided, may become useful men and women. These children are not from the slums of the city, many never saw New York City. They are from various Orphanages in the state.

Persons taking the children must treat them in every way as members of the family, send them to school, church, Sunday school, and properly clothe them, until they are 18 years of age. It is then expected that they will receive some wages.

The following well-known citizens have kindly consented to act as a committee to aid the agent in securing homes:

| J. A. HOWARD | MATTIE LEE A. LAIR | R. M. ESTES |
| A. N. TRAVIS | A. F. METELMAN | J. T. HODGES |

Distribution will take place at the Court House

10 A. M., Friday, September 23

An address will be given by the agent. Persons desiring to take children are requested to give their names to the committee as early as possible. Applicants must be endorsed by local committee. All are invited.

Office: 105 East 22d St., New York City.

H. D. CLARK, Iowa Agent,
Dodge Center, Minn.

Dodger for the Sidney, Iowa distribution of September 22, 1904.

(top). Alice Quince.

(bottom). Florence Volkhart at age thirteen.

OSCEOLA, IOWA - OCTOBER 20th, 1904

Some children placed were:
Letitia Achers- "Lutie Pearsons" (first placed in Tamora, Nebraska in
   1903)
Boy-Albrecht
Boy-Albrecht
Effie May Bennett (see "Guardianships")
Emma Creter (replaced in 1905 with Christoph Muller of Griswold,
   Iowa)
James Decker
Jennie Decker
William Decker
Tracy Emick (placed with Clarence E. Carder)
Mabel Hartwock
Boy-Hartwock
Boy-Hartwock
Boy-Hartwock
Ida Johnson
Archie K. (age two)
Helen Kitchen
Henrietta Kitchen (placed with Gordon family)
Arthur L.
Paul Medler
Rosa Moyan
Harold Oakes (replaced at Strawberry Point, Iowa)
Charles Wirth (placed in Murray, Iowa with his brother, Edward)
Edward Wirth

This was an unusually fine distribution and there were so many
applications for children that I kept bringing wards there for a long
time. There were several unusually good children in this company.
Some boys served in the World War.
   Emma Creter was a fine German girl, innocent and well
mannered. She was born October 20th, 1891 in Brooklyn, New York.

She went back out east to relatives in New York City on March 12th, 1909.

Two of the most beautiful children were William and Jennie Decker. Jennie was exceptionally fine, became an active Christian, married and died at Dodge City. James Decker did not do well.

Tracy Emick was born May 19th, 1902. He enlisted for the World War and was in the Anti-Aircraft Regiment, Battery "E." He was discharged January 3rd, 1923. His address in 1923 was Oakland, California.

Mabel Hartwock did not know her birthday, but she selected July 4th. She was a very active girl, but stubborn. She had three brothers, but they had to be returned to New York.

Ida Johnson of the New Sharon Company was replaced here and was one of the finest Swede girls I ever had. She was born November 15th, 1899. She graduated from High School and taught successfully for some time. She was raised by some old people who loved her greatly. She married in Osceola to a Mr. J. H. Daniels, farmer, on February 5th, 1921.

I brought two girls to Osceola from Nebraska. Helen and Henrietta Kitchen, whose mother in New York writes me her gratitude for not separating her daughters. Henrietta was born January 14th, 1904. She was first placed at Plainview, Nebraska in 1909 and then in Osceola, Iowa on October 11th, 1910. They became teachers I think.

Rosa Moyan was born November 23rd, 1895. She was an Italian. She was placed first at Greenwood, Nebraska on November 7th, 1903 with Catholics. She was placed last at Osceola and adopted as "Rosa Baker" in 1907. There was given her anything that money could buy at her first home, but she would not call them mama and papa, and did not want to stay with them, so they gave her up. She was playing with her gifts on Christmas morning 1903 when I reached her home and took her away (I am writing of this on another Christmas, 1921). I took her to a Methodist family on a farm in Tamora, Nebraska. This family had previously taken a little girl named Ida E. Cook (She was a girl wanting constant entertainment and attention. She, at five years of age, could ask enough questions to "drive one crazy" as they say. By request, I had replaced her where she apparently did well and grew up. I never saw Miss Ida again, until eight years later, when visiting in the state.) Rosa was very opposite of Ida, a quiet and tractable child, just what the family had asked for. Although, in three months, I received a request to come and remove her. The foster mother said she could never love another child except the first one turned away. I then placed Rosa with a Seventh Day Adventist family at Seward, Nebraska, but the woman was not strong and also had a petted boy. I again had to remove Rosa. I made arrangements to place her with a physician at North Loup, Nebraska and was about to send a man after her when I was informed that another agent had been there and taken her into Missouri on a farm. Rosa wrote me one or two letters and then ceased. After two years, I had a letter from the M.E. pastor of her foster parents, and an agent of a Missouri Home. He said she was fearfully abused and that I ought to remove her. I went there (Rockport, Missouri) and had two days of parlaying, and not succeeding in finding what was the matter, I consented to let her stay, the foster mother pleading and weeping. I no sooner had done this than the pastor and town were "up in arms" against my decision. I went to some neighbors and to a brother of this man, who also had taken a ward, and all I could get out of them was, "Don't wish to get mixed up in it, but you'd better remove the child." I was then determined to remove her at any cost and so the next day I went there and found them at the dinner table and with company. I said, "Madam, I have changed my mind since yesterday and I think I'll have to take the child away." Then the fire flew!

In a rage she said, "You shall not take her, you are a fraud and a villain and a liar! You are not an agent of the Society!"

I replied, "Madam, you can not call me a villain in your own house. I have papers here giving me authority to remove this girl. Yesterday, you did not object my authority, nor question it. I want and must have that girl and you get her clothes ready for her." The girl was eating with her head downcast and looked as though she had not a friend on earth.

"Madam, you turn that girl over to me at once, you are not a fit woman to have the girl," I said.

"I'll make you prove that, sir," she replied.

"All right, I'll prove that in ten minutes in town. Hitch up your horse and come down, but I'll have the child before I go."

I stepped to the table and took Rosa away and led her to the carriage and we took our seats, the man following me and the woman screaming and in a rage. I turned to the man and said, "You bring this child's clothes to me in town before I leave or I'll send the Sheriff after you," and I drove off.

At about sundown, he came with two bundles of clothes and cried like a child, wanting to see her. I let her go to him a moment and he asked if he could write to her. "No sir, it would not be proper just now and would be unjust to her new foster parents. You can never know where I take her, but I am not blaming you, it is your wife that is to blame and I pity you." He kissed the child and went away. She was then eleven years of age. She was adopted by a farmer who also had had a girl I once placed with him and had removed. Here she stayed happy and contented until about twenty years old. They bought her a piano and she became a leader in song and music. I annually called on her and her folks. One time, during a visit in about 1910 and after hearing her sing in church, I asked her as we walked to her home, "Rosa, this is not much like the day I kidnapped you in Missouri, is it?"

"No, she said laughing, "but I carry the marks of that Missouri home to this day."

I do not know what those marks were. They moved from the farm to town, building a pretty new house. I visited them in April of 1915 and on September 5th, 1921 I visited her and her husband in Chicago. She spoke gratefully of my rescuing her and what I had done for her welfare. She was married to a Mr. George A. Trendle in 1919.

Charles Wirth was born December 22nd, 1892 and Edward was born September 26th, 1897.

(top). Lutie Achers (l) and Rosa Moyan (r).

(bottom). Emma Creter.

(top). Tracy Emick at her foster home.

(bottom). Helen (r) and Henrietta (l) Kitchen.

Charles Worth (l) and Edward Worth (r).

LEON, IOWA - NOVEMBER 18th, 1904

Some children placed were:
Martha Virginia Bennett "Bertha Peck" (placed with Edwin M. Peck
  of Decatur, Iowa)
Jennie Decker
Boy-Decker
Boy-Decker
Ethel May Duncan (placed with Mrs. Fred Orchard of Decatur, Iowa)
Madeline H.
Nora H.
Marian Kelleran
Wilbur (Main?)
Maggie Remore

This was a year of special attention to Iowa, though a few visits and replacings were had in other states. About as usual there. Some very nice and pretty children. We received for placing quite a number from the Ogdensburgh, New York Home, but these seemed to be below the average and unable to keep good homes. They did not seem to have the right start from the orphanage they came from. The cause of this I did not study. Two of these were brother and sister and were incorrigible. This girl however had brains and talents worthy a better use than she gave them at first. I have not followed their history and am unable to tell the results.

Martha Virginia Bennett "Bertha Peck" was born May 23rd, 1903. She was later adopted.

We had a sister and two brothers named Decker from "respectable stock" who were placed through unfortunate circumstances. The oldest brother was a pretty boy, but he did not turn out well. He had a checkered career. The youngest had a good Christian home, but too indulgent and he grew headstrong and uncontrollable. It ought not to be. Every child is entitled to wholesome and firm home government and it is a great mistake to call overindulgence like good old Eli's love. It is not true love for the child, it is lack of sense, and the realization of a child's rights. The right to be well brought up, law abiding and confiding. The girl was a very handsome one and well trained in a Seventh Day Adventist home. She became a fine Christian woman and often wrote me in a religious and joyful strain. I visited her in April of 1915 and she was married in June. She had one child and died in faith.

Ethel May Duncan was born August 25th, 1898. She was later replaced in Osceola and Greenfield, Iowa and was last placed February 27th, 1906 in Milford, Nebraska with Riley and Jennie Wright. She married Roy Stolz of Milford on February 20th, 1917. They moved to Des Moines, Iowa and then to Crete, Nebraska and again to Des Moines. They have several children.

We had one splendid baby. Her name was later changed to Berta P. A. Kelleran. She was later returned to New York and the House of Mercy.

Wilber (Main?), a stady and industrious boy who made good. He went to a farmer who several times attempted to be rid of him, but his wife saw the possibilities of the boy and his desirability (and her own responsibility). The greatest trouble was her husband's fierce temper, and so she held on to the boy, writing for me not to pay attention to the man!

Maggie Remore was a desirable girl in many respects, but somehow her relatives secured her back and not for her good apparently. She did not want to return.

We had three in this company that I brought from other Iowa towns for replacing. They were disappointments. I have mentioned them elsewhere.

(top). Martha V. Bennett.

(bottom). Martha V. Bennett at her foster home.

Ethel May Duncan with inset photo of her foster mother.

Distributions

LENOX AND OAKLAND, IOWA - FRIDAY, DECEMBER 9th, 1904

Some children placed in Oakland were:
Alice Quince (see also Sidney, Iowa distribution)
Bella Quince (see also Sidney, Iowa distribution)
James Ryan (placed with C. H. Powell)
Lawrence Shanne
William Shanne

Some children placed in Lenox were:
Dorothy Comstock
Clara Neilbren (later placed in Nebraska)
Eva May Seaman (twin)-(placed with Lizzie Hegwood-see also
  Sidney, Iowa distribution)
Leonard Wilson (placed with S. E. Wainwright)

This was another double distribution that I had arranged. We divided the company at a point on the Burlington Road. Mr. Tice took the Lenox children, while I went on to Oakland. This Oakland distribution took place in the Opera House. While enroute to Oakland we reached Carson too late to catch the train and would have had to wait until the next day, so I proceeded with a livery with all the children. Later on I had to make a visit to Lenox, as there were some difficulties there that I had to straighten out.

I had one little boy with a most vicious disposition. He insisted on chewing up his shoe strings and kicking out his shoes on the irons of the car seats. I gave him three good spankings, which at last seemed to subdue him, but while I was after the livery he was so mean with the other children that when I returned I had to take off my overcoat and give him a threshing. The people in the station did not understand the situation and had much sympathy with the child. He was simply a tiger. That night the boy slept with me and he put his arms about me and said, "I love you Mr. Clarke. I will be a good boy." Later that boy inherited a part of a New Jersey farm and went back to be trained in his inheritance. I trust he was trained to overcome his inheritance.

190

At Lenox were several quite interesting placings. Baby Dorothy Comstock went to Corning and was adopted.

I had the two Quince girls to replace. They sang for me at a meeting where I spoke in the Methodist Church on Sunday evening. I was taken suddenly ill and had to telegraph Mr. Tice to come and I went home and was very sick for two weeks. I was then sent for to take the Quince's away from a German home where they had been placed. The foster parents came and left them at a hotel and hastened back home just before my train arrived. The poor girls were clean and nice when placed and were very proud ones. When I arrived I found them very unclean and they said they had not had a bath in all that time. They were also with the itch and their hair was full of the biggest bugs I ever saw. The doctor called it the Philippine itch. In that condition I had to take them to other towns and replace them, where they were cured.

James Ryan was born April 13th, 1897.

We had with us one of the twins from the Sidney company and she did well (Eva Seaman). Once, on my visit there, a dog tried to eat me up and succeeded in getting a small part of one leg. A free use of stones and sticks won me the day. On another occasion elsewhere, I was attacked by a vicious dog that bit me twice and made me lame for some time. The foster mother of the wards did a good job with bandages and ointment.

There were two brothers that were interesting in my Oakland company, William and Lawrence Shanne. They had just come from a dying mother who had left them with prayers for their placing. I could never get them into communication with me after visiting them in the new homes. There was something strange about them. They kept their homes and grew up in the community. I cannot take space to tell all the history of their placing.

Leonard Wilson was born June 8th, 1902. He was from the Chappauqua Sanitarium. He had a sister Ida in the Elizabeth Home in New York. Leonard was taken by a Presbyterian minister whose wife left him and he was replaced with a lumberman. And so on.

Chicago, Milwaukee & St.Paul
RAILWAY.   1905

Pass Rev. H. D. Clarke

Agent Children's Aid Society.

DURING THE CURRENT YEAR UPON CONDITIONS ON BACK HEREOF

Nº 1902.   CHAIRMAN.

Railroad Pass used by Reverend Mr. Clarke for the year 1905.

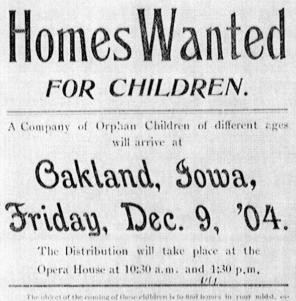

Homes Wanted

FOR CHILDREN.

A Company of Orphan Children of different ages
will arrive at

Oakland, Iowa,
Friday, Dec. 9, '04.

The Distribution will take place at the
Opera House at 10:30 a.m. and 1:30 p.m.

The object of the coming of these children is to find homes in your midst, especially among farmers, where they may enjoy a happy and wholesome family life, where kind care, good example and moral training will fit them for a life of self-support and usefulness. They come under the auspices of the New York Children's Aid Society, by whom they have been tested and found to be well-meaning and willing boys and girls.

The conditions are that these children shall be properly clothed, treated as members of the family, given proper school advantages and remain in the family until they are eighteen years of age. At the expiration of the time specified it is hoped that arrangements can be made whereby they may be able to remain in the family indefinitely. The Society retains the right to remove a child at any time for just cause and agrees to remove any found unsatisfactory after being notified.

Applications may be made to any one of the following well known citizens, who have agreed to act as local committee to aid the agent in securing homes.

Committee: S. S. Rust, E. M. Smart, A. C. Vieth, E. C. Read, W. B. Butler, Dr. R. G. Smith, N. W. Wentz.

Remember the time and place. All are invited.
Come out and hear the address.

Office: 105 East 22d St., New York City.

H. D. CLARK, Iowa Agent,
Dodge Center, Minn.

Dodger for the Oakland, Iowa distribution of December 9, 1904.

(top). Eva May Seaman on February 10, 1913.

(bottom). James Ryan at age fourteen. Photo taken September 1, 1911.

Leonard Wilson.

MAYSVILLE AND ROCK PORT, MISSOURI - JANUARY 19th, 1905

<u>Some children placed Maysville were</u>:
Anna Huber (age six)
Freda Huber
Benjamin Magnus (age fourteen)
George Neary
Harold Neary
Lillie Neary

<u>Some children placed in Rock Port were</u>:
Harry Apgar
Meta Clausen (replaced at Mattawan, Minnesota)
Samuel Connett
Sarah Connett
Irving Cooley
Martin Cooley
Franklin Cummings
Lettie Greason
Alfred Gunderson
Frederick Gunderson
Mamie Gunderson (see photo on p. 345)
Andrew Koovasteeh
Rosa Moyan (replaced March 26th, 1907 with A. N. Baker of
  Osceola, Iowa-see also Osceola, Iowa distribution)
Daniel Webster
Bennie Wilson
Elwood Ziener

I could not attend this distribution personally. I later visited the wards here. It was here that I replaced the Rosa Moyan from Nebraska with whom I had such a time removing.

Meta Clauson was born January 28th, 1894. I later on took her to Dodge Center, Minnesota and paid for her board until an appropriate home was found for her. She was a very pretty and healthy Swede girl and was placed in several homes, where she had troubles of various kinds; most often, but not always her own fault. She had quite a history. Mr. Tice came there to take her back to New York City, but Mrs. Clarke would not let her go and succeeded in placing her and she was then hired out at wages. She was married March 18th, 1915 to an Owatonna man who was a successful baggageman of the C. M. & St. Paul Road and later the Rock Island Railway. His name was Charles Wallace. I visited her in July of that year. I visited again in September, 1915 when passing through the town and lastly on October 12th, 1925. She developed into a handsome woman and is still at work. She often comes to see me and she tells me she is very grateful for being saved from being taken back to the Elizabeth Home for girls. One of our active Seventh Day Baptist church sisters interested herself in Meta and lets her come any time and call her place home when she is out of work.

It was from Rock Port that I snatched away the Italian girl mentioned elsewhere, placing her at Osceola, Iowa.

One most interesting case was that of Miss Mamie Gunderson of Rock Port. She was on a farm and a member of the family was a President or Professor of a College somewhere in Missouri. This girl was an excellent scholar and was hungry for a higher education. She wanted me to give her such an opportunity and with the consent of her foster parents I took her to one of our Seventh Day Baptist College towns (Milton, Wisconsin) and sent her through High School. She graduated at the head of her class. She had worked for her board by caring for two little children. She was a most beautiful young woman and very winning. A strong, healthy and hard working one. In 1913, when I was Superintendent of the Haskell Home at Battle Creek, Michigan, I made her Assistant Matron and she was most excellent help, kind and patient with the children and never grumbled over extra work. She endeared herself to all by her winning ways and lovely disposition. She returned to Milton and completed her course, graduating at the head of her class. In the summer of 1914, she returned to Battle Creek for employment in the Sanitarium and in the fall she entered Milton College with a scholarship. She had bright prospects intellectually, but had a hard struggle financially. She had refused an offer of marriage and began to keep company with another young man who seemed to worship the ground she walked on, but he was not worthy of her and I cautioned her not to give him encouragement unless she "meant business." She broke it off, but during the holiday vacation in 1914 she went back to Rock Port to visit her brother and became acquainted on short notice with a young man and engaged herself to marry him. She asked me for advice. I told her it would lead her away from her church and that she had not proved him yet, being too hasty. She seemed to resent it and went in early August of 1915 and married him. She never wrote to me again. I lost all track of her. I could not blame her for some things in her struggles to work her way through college. Mr. Brace offered to help her and advised the Normal as taking less time and expense before being fitted for teaching. Mr. Brace wrote to me February 11th, 1915:

"Dear Mr. Clarke,

I have yours of the 5th . . . I am glad that you saw Mamie Gunderson when in Milton (Wisconsin). She seems to be an extremely nice girl and I do not blame her for getting tired of struggling to keep at the top of her class when the hard work made it impossible to do so. I had $25.00 for her and could have raised more for this year if it had been necessary . . . I could not, however, raise $55.00 for four years . . . Mamie has not given up the idea of completing her education. I advised the Normal College because it would only take a year, and would fit her to become a teacher, or else a course in library work if she could find the proper place to take it . . . I advised her to write to the public library at Minneapolis, to find out the best school. I am waiting now to hear whether I am to keep this $25.00 until next fall to add to what she has saved or whether I shall spend it on somebody else . . . Mamie has great affection for you, and appreciates very much what you have done for her.

Yours very truly,

R. N. Brace, Supt."

This case made me very sad, for I had been as a father to her. She was a girl of remarkable promise for usefulness, but it developed that she had little deep religious convictions and what she was religiously, was just for the occasion where she happened to be. In High School and College life, so few young people seriously study the religious principles they have espoused, and the selection of a profession or life work often overshadows all else. Mamie had two brothers placed in Missouri, one of whom later went to Nebraska.

Some of my most promising wards whom I came to love dearly, have been a disappointment to me, but time may change them for the better.

Meta Clausen.

MAXWELL, IOWA - MAY 18th, 1905

Some children placed were:
Mary Barrett (see Manilla, Iowa distribution)
Gertrude L. Bell "Iris Arrington" (placed with Frank and Sarah
 Arrington of Welton, Iowa)
David DaLara "Fred Randlette" (placed with David Randlette)
Fanny DaLara
Cora DeRocher
Henry Gillenly (from Greenfield, Iowa)
Homer Hayden (later went to Nebraska)
Willie Hayden (placed with Otto Thomas of Traer, Iowa)
Allen Hermance
Charles Hermance (placed on a farm with A. S. Gifford)
Francis Hermance (placed with Mrs. John Brodie)
Edward Highbrown
Eleanor Ogden
Maggie Estella Remore (see also Leon, Iowa distribution)
Minnie Wade (see also Oelwein, Iowa)
Edward Willard

This company was one of special interest and some of the
wards made extra good. Miss Anna L. Hill was with me and had
charge of an extra fine baby I had reserved for special friends among
Seventh Day Baptists at Welton, Iowa. Her name was Gertrude L.
Bell. She was just two days short of being two years old, being born
May 20th, 1903. She came from the Sheltering Arms Nursery of
Brooklyn, New York. She was left there by her mother on August
12th, 1903. Her father's name was George and her mother's name was
Lillian. She was received by the Children's Aid Society on March 15th,
1905. She was legally adopted by Frank and Sarah Arrington. Her
foster sister there was Olga Arrington, a very talented girl; an artist,
poet and lover of birds, as well as Church organist. She was a very
active and useful young woman. Gertrude Arrington studied music and
became a proficient teacher of such in Chicago and at home.

Fanny and David DaLara were French. David was born in 1900. David was a good boy and went to Missouri with foster parents. Fannie was born December 14th, 1895. She was a very obstinate girl and disobedient. She was pretty, but could not get acclimated to homes, though I found her two homes of some wealth. At last, she returned to her first home. She later married, but divorced her husband and I lost all track of her.

Cora DeRocher was French. I had reserved her for a German family who had already taken one of our wards, Augusta Heilman. Cora is now in the care of the Devos family of Spring Valley, Minnesota. She was a sweet child and the shyest little midget I ever saw, being exceedingly afraid of men. I had her with me for several days on railway journeys and held her much. She married twice and has one boy named Lawrence and a set of twins. I at last put her in communication with her sisters in the east and she had a joyful visit with them later on.

Henry Gillenly went to Greenfield, Iowa and then came back to Maxwell, and later was sent back to New York City.

The Hermance brothers were fine boys. Frances was born October 21st, 1898. He became a member of the Maxwell Cornet Band and enlisted in the World War and died July 12th, 1924. He had married in 1920 and his widow lives in Sioux City, Iowa. The other two became good farmers. Charles Hermance was born May 29th, 1897. He was in the World War and served with the Ambulance Corps in France. He married at Maxwell. A fine letter of affection and appreciation for being placed in a good home was received in 1922. The oldest clung to me especially and was having a hard struggle, but I kept him encouraged. They had another brother named Robert.

Homer Hayden had strenuous times at a place in Nebraska. Willie Hayden was born December 22nd, 1896. He later moved to Waterloo, Iowa.

Edward Highbrown was taken to Afton, Iowa, but was later also returned to New York City.

Eleanor Ogden had to be returned to New York City. She had been deserted by her stepfather and mother. She had two very brief homes at Maxwell, Iowa.

Maggie Remore was worthy of a good home, but her father obtained an order from the court and she was returned to his miserable home against her wishes.

Minnie Wade had to be replaced several times all over the state. She gradually developed into a strange acting and abnormal girl, false in speech and purpose. It would be horrible to relate her words and acts in print. She was taken back for discipline, but a stepmother obtained her, saving her from a Reformatory perhaps. The stepmother attempted a lawsuit with me over her case, but having no grounds for it, her threat was never noticed and she was soon lost sight of. Minnie had lots of trouble with a very bad temper, but withal, was innocent and in need of great sympathy.

Edward Willard was a Catholic. One evening he went out to shoot sparrows and not seeing his foster father in the barn door, accidentally shot him, putting out an eye. The poor man was taken to Mercy Hospital at Des Moines, Iowa. It was a great grief to the boy, but was carelessness, not planned. He was so frightened that he ran away and that made the people in the community think he did it purposely, but such was not the case and his foster father said it was an accident. But the neighborhood was so wrought up that the boy had to leave and I placed him with a Protestant man at wages. I could not find a Catholic home for him. After he was old enough he went back to New York City and then to Delaware. I have lost sight of him.

Iris Arrington with her foster mother.

Mary Barrett.

(top). Fanny and David DaLara

(bottom). Cora DeRocher.

Willie Hayden with foster parents.

Frank and Charles Hermance.

Edward Willard.

Some children placed were:
Hugo Anderson
Edith Anderson
Mary Anderson (placed with Dr. R. H. Watson and adopted)
Sadie Brooks (replaced January 23rd, 1908 with W. E. and Mary
  Sanders of Olewein, Iowa)
Cecil Davis
John Doer
Frances Narr (placed with C. E. Boutwell and went to Reverend C. C.
  Hatchen in Savannah, Missouri in 1911)
Grace Narr (placed with Alma Howard)
Lester Narr (placed with C. E. Boutwell)
Claude Tomlinson (placed in Kingston, Missouri)
Mary Tomlinson "Margaret Waggoner" (placed with W. J. Waggoner
  of Kingston, Missouri)
Willie Tomlinson (replaced by Mr. Swan)
August Zeman
Edward Zeman
Stephen Zeman

This was a thrilling town on the C. B. and Q. Railway. The placings were good, with one or two exceptions. The company was mostly made up of a number of brothers and sisters, with quite strong attachments.

Three Andersons, a brother and two sisters, had a strenuous time. They were from the Staten Island Nursery and Hospital. One poor sister had to be returned east. A doctor took the other two. Mary Anderson "Marie Watson" was born September 29th, 1899. The foster father was too prominent in the community to suit the tax payers, who did not want a certain roads and bridges built so as to increase taxes. In revenge they coaxed the boy away from him. It was with great difficulty that I secured the boy and as a result, I had to take him far away. Later, he was sent to Arkansas, where he obtained a good education. The original foster family moved to Oklahoma. The girl was adopted by the mother after a separation of doctor and wife. She was about to settle a part of the estate upon the girl, but the law forbade that without the husband's consent, unless they were divorced. Pending all this, the doctor came back, made up with them and they moved to Texas. They later refused to make any reports of her. The girl did not want anyone to know she was only an adopted girl and for that reason, did not want the agent to make her any visits!

Sadie Brooks had been an abandoned girl. She was born December 16th, 1899. She went to Oelwein, Iowa and then to Stuttgart, Arkansas. She was called "Mildred."

Cecil Davis was returned to New York by mistake and was returned and I replaced him twice.

John Doer was illegally kidnapped as it were, but as he was large enough to soon look out for his interests, I declined to rescue him from the farmer who wanted him so badly.

A Narr boy and two sisters were fine and the girls had educational advantages and grew up with some hard experiences, but surmounted them all. Frances was born January 30th, 1894. She married C. Ciesler in Kansas City, Missouri in 1916. Grace was born November 20th, 1898. In 1925 she was with her sister Frances and in poor health. Lester was born July 16th, 1897. He was married and later separated. He has one child. Lester and his oldest sister, Frances, were placed together on a farm. Some very interesting correspondence has been had from Frances.

Mary Tomlinson was a sweet girl and had three homes, but not from her own faults. She was a very winsome lass and very affectionate, though strong in will. I had some startling experiences in placing her. Her foster parents were quite faulty, though well to do and respectable. After about three years a misunderstanding between him and his wife caused a replacing. I replaced her and then the family wanted her back again. The child was almost heartbroken over being replaced. Before I could interfere, the first foster parent had gone after her and taken her back, but suddenly decided not to have her after she had gotten there. She was left at a place and I came back and replaced her. At last adopted by a farmer named Waggoner, she grew up a well educated woman and married well. Her brother was also a bright and industrious boy and succeeded as a farmer. He owns a ranch in the far west. In 1913, he wrote me one of the most appreciative letters I ever received from a boy. It was very long and full of affection and confidence in telling his plans for the future.

(top). Grace Narr.

(bottom). Lester Narr.

(top). Frances Narr.

(bottom). Mary Tomlinson.

Claude Tomlinson.

STRAWBERRY POINT, IOWA - SEPTEMBER 21st, 1905

<u>Some children placed were</u>:

Edith Anderson (sister of Mary and Hugo of the Hamilton, Missouri distribution)

Gertrude Chambers (age about eight, placed with Mrs. M. E. Taylor)

John Davis "John Henderson"

Henry F.

Harold Growther

Florence Heulman (placed with Mrs. Fred Densmore of Edgewood, Iowa)

Edna Kingsland (age about nine, placed with E. F. Parish of Mederville, Iowa)

Harry Kingsland (placed later in same home as above)

Walter Kingsland (age five, placed in same home as above)

Mary Jane Scollons

    I had Edith Anderson at Hamilton, Missouri. She was a sister of two children placed there. I placed her with her sister, but they wouldn't keep her and I had to remove her. I again had to take her to Stanberry, Missouri, where the courts took her away from her foster father on complaint of a teacher. I went to make investigation and found he had committed no crime and so I took the girl into Iowa, where she could not be a witness against him. He then had the impudence to write me, wanting her back again. She stayed in northeastern Iowa several years. She was not as bright as some.

    Gertrude Chambers was taken by a Mrs. Taylor, a wealthy widow lady, and raised by her. When the girl was ten or eleven years old I took her to the Mayo surgeons at Rochester, Minnesota for removal of tonsils, with the operation being free. I was privileged to watch the operation, which was against the rules. Operations were often gratis for the poor. I kept the girl near my home for a few days and then took her back to her foster mother, who was able to pay for a dozen operations. This cost her nothing except the child's fare and a week's care at two dollars a week. My time and expense was not charged her, as I offered to do it free. I have never had any acts of appreciation for this since. Mrs. Taylor left her some bank stock, but Gertrude married against her will to a poor man that she loved and lives happily with. She was not to have the legacy until she was thirty-five years of age. To obtain this, Gertrude asked me to get a birth certificate for her, as her foster mother had without any authority, put her age back two years from what it was, as given by the Aid Society. No birth certificate could be found anywhere in New York State, as I wrote all the offices where records are made for the city and state of New York. That seemed so strange. I did not hear from her for many years, but in April of 1928, Gertrude wrote to tell me that the bank failed that held her legacy and all was lost. She now lives in Chicago.

John Davis came from Canesteo, New York. He had a few good homes. One at Skyberry, Minnesota. His father was George Henderson of Paseo, Washington on the steamboat "Mountain Gem." John was returned to his stepsister in Hornell, New York.

Henry F. had a various experience and then went to Delaware.

Florence Heulman was born about 1900. She came from the Nursery and Child's Hospital at Staten Island, New York. She was taken by a family of wealth at Edgwood, Iowa and soon did not know she was not their own child. She never knew she was the object of my visits. She was a very pretty, fascinating German child. They later moved to Long Beach, California. She was legally adopted in 1907 and her foster mother asked me not to inform her. She will, however, hear the truth from some source in time, as they always do. It is not wise to try to keep the situation from a child for too long. I used to visit one girl who did not know she was adopted until age sixteen. She was told she had two grown sisters nearby who were teachers and they had been kept from seeing her. She went into a serious fever. Others have turned against the foster parents for thus keeping the facts from them.

There were two brothers and a sister named Kingsland. The older brother came later and all went to one home, which was unusual. Edna was born April 7th, 1896. Harry was born October 8th, 1892 and Walter was born August 31st, 1900. They were all from the Five Points House of Industry in New York.

Mary Jane Scollons came from the Wadena company of 1904 and while working out was taken seriously ill and died at Mrs. M. E. Taylor's.

(next page). The Strawberry Point, Iowa company. In back: John Davis (left) and Edith Anderson (right). Center row (left to right): Edna Kingsland, H. D. Clarke and Gertrude Chambers. Front row (left to right): Harold Growther, Walter Kingsland and Florence Heulman.

Florence Heulman.

Left to right: Harry, Edna and Walter Kingsland.

STANBERRY, MISSOURI - OCTOBER 26th, 1905

Some children placed were:
Elizabeth Hagen (age six, placed with J. B. Denham of Gentry, Missouri)
Walter Hagen (age two and a half)
Christopher Kultz (age four)
John Rapp (age three and a half, placed with sister below, but later removed)
Lucy "Louise" Rapp
Alice Robinson (see Princeton, Missouri distribution)
Herbert Robinson (age nine)
Willie Robinson (age four and a half)

This was a small party. I was alone with this, having no helper for the girls. This town was the headquarters of the Church of God, a denomination of Sabbath keepers. I made many friends here and had a successful distribution. Later, I brought more into the community, but the most of them were subsequently replaced. Jacob Brinkerhoff and wife, whom I had known at Alfred, New York years ago, were the editors of the denominational paper at Stanberry.

Walter and Lizzie Hagen, brother and sister, were taken by a Church of God family and raised in that faith. Lizzie was born June 13th, 1899. Lizzie married Fred Poff of Stanberry and went to Glasgow, Montana and Fort William, Ontario and then returned to Stanberry. Her husband died at Fort William from the smoke of a burning house, leaving her with two children. She wrote to me for help. At last, she was lost track of and no word could be received. In 1926 Lizzie was searching for her brother Walter, with whom she'd lost touch. She found him and he went to visit her at Fort William.

John and Louise Rapp were French. Their father was Frank and their mother was Lizzie Metzger. The father was an expressman. Both parents were born in Germany and were Protestants. There is another sister named Margaret at the New York Infant Asylum. I placed Louise and John together, but Louise was later given up. She was a very sweet child and took her abandonment very sorrowfully. She was born September 5th, 1900. She was replaced again in January, 1908 with S. C. and Matilda Linn of Newtown, Missouri. She was adopted as "Bertie Linn" and the family moved to Ravanna, Missouri in October 1908. On April 9th, 1920 she was at Wichita, Kansas. John Rapp died young.

The Robinson children were from the Binghamton, New York Orphan's Home. The parents were separated and the mother went to an Alms House. Willie was placed on a farm at Stanberry and was later replaced in two different homes in Afton, Iowa. Herbert was also placed at Stanberry. He was born at Owego, New York. On April 1st, 1906 I took Willie and Alice to see him. He was also replaced at Afton, Iowa. He had also been at Cresco and Oakland, Iowa, where he ran away. They have a brother Henry at Plattsburg, Missouri.

Elizabeth Hagen.

Louise and John Rapp.

Distributions

DE WITT, IOWA - JANUARY 4th, 1906

Some children placed were:
Fred Hayden (age five)
Alpha Hill (age three and a half, placed with George Henderson)
Florence Kahnis (age six)
Jennie McIntosh (age sixteen)
Elsie Pape (age seven)
Harry Pape (age eleven and a half)
George Reynolds (age four)
Jesse Reynolds (age five)
Ira Shengo (age six and a half)
Kenneth Swayz (age eighteen months)
Floyd Townsend (age three, placed with Albert Haney and replaced in 1907/8 with Mr. Denison in De Witt, Iowa)
James Willis (age four and a half)

Miss Anna L. Hill was assisting me with this distribution. A number of these were adopted. Nothing special to record of these, being like the rest, except that I had a Scotch girl of sixteen years named Jennie McIntosh that I had promised to people near her two brothers in Missouri. I had to go and replace her in Iowa however. She was a very nice young woman, had a good disposition and was a hard worker, but she evidently had an insane sulk at times. One instance: She was asked to pare some potatoes and ordinarily would have done it willingly, but all at once she refused and went to her room and stayed there for two days without food. When she came down she was as sweet as ever, as though nothing had happened. Had the family kept her and paid no attention to the sulks, few and far between, she would have served them well and come to no harm, but they turned her off. An absent uncle of hers in Brooklyn, who had not been heard of in many years, turned up and wanted her. She was sent back. In a few months she had her sulks and was turned out of her uncle's house, homeless and alone. She wrote to me and I could have saved her, but she gave me no address and so I could never get at her to help. She was never heard from again. The poor lost girl. Her mother I believe had been insane.

Alfred (or Alpha) Hill was born September 14th, 1901. No history. He was loved in his home, but he died in September, 1914 at De Witt.

Florence Kahnis was a cute, uneasy, active girl and would not have been kept in most homes, but she fell into good hands. She was replaced in Princeton, Missouri. She was never still a moment when awake. Her foster father was an undertaker and furniture dealer. He often opened his combination safe in her presence and she had closely watched it. He permitted her to play with the money often. She seemed honest and never took a thing until one day when he was away she, with her keen sharp eyes, had observed the combination and opened the safe and stole thirty dollars. She carried it to school and the scholars twitted her of stealing and that frightened her. She hid part of the money under the board walk and threw the rest away into the grass. The foster mother questioned her and together they went and found all the money. She was then ten years of age. They moved far out west later on and she was growing up into a beautiful promising life. When in Prado, California in June of 1917 she was horseback when her horse ran away. Both were killed by a passing train.

Elsie and Harry Pape were brother and sister. They were peculiar children, but seemed to retain their homes. Harry grew up a good boy and man. He was a farmer near Welton. Elsie went to a city home in Clinton, Iowa. She always seemed so afraid of me when I visited her home. Evidently she had taken something that was not hers and they had told her threateningly that if she did not do right they would send for me to take her. I could never gain her confidence, though I tried hard to assure her that I did not want to remove her and should not, unless her folks compelled me, but it was no use. That was a common threat against orphan children. She stayed in her home and in 1915 I visited her at Clinton.

The Reynolds brothers were very handsome boys. They were placed together and we all thought it a great success, but trouble soon began and I had to replace them. Jesse was a bright child and after a while I settled him with a nice German family with no children and he has won their hearts. George has not been so fortunate.

The baby Kenneth Swayze was adopted and taken to Monticello, Iowa. His parents were unknown. I last heard from him in 1915.

Floyd Townsend was born February 19th, 1903.

James Willis was from Sheltering Arms Nursery in Brooklyn, New York. His parents were dead. He was later adopted.

The following article ran in the *Clinton Weekly Herald* on January 6, 1906:

De Witt, Jan. 4 -

The company of children that were to be here Thursday arrived at 9:30 by way of Delmar. There were ten in the party. They were accompanied by Mr. Clarke and Miss Hill and were a bright and intelligent lot of little ones, ages ranging from 16 years to 18 months. Author's note: (The Children's names, ages and where placed was listed next).

There are three that are not yet placed - Kenneth Swayz, 18 months; Fred Hayden, 5 years and Ira Shengo, 6 1/2 years.

Mr. Clark expects to stay in this city for a few days and hopes to find homes for the last three. He can be found at Sheldon's Boarding House.

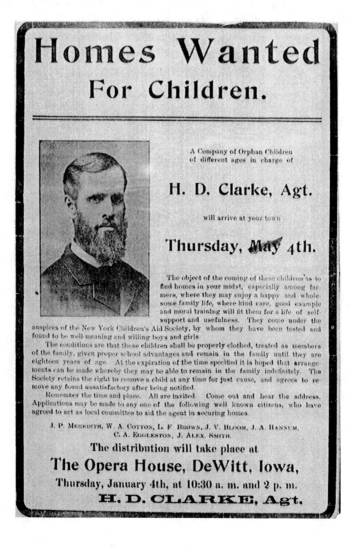

Dodger for the Dewitt, Iowa distribution of January 4, 1906.

(top). Alfred Hill.

(bottom). Florence Kahnis.

George and Jesse Reynolds with foster parents and foster sisters.

Floyd Townsend.

PRINCETON, MISSOURI - JANUARY 18th, 1906

<u>Some children placed were</u>:
Bertha Beckman
Leo Burning (age four)
Beatrice Chadwick (placed with M. F. Robinson, a banker)
Isadore Ethel Doyle (age ten)
James Doyle (age seven)
Florence Kahnis (see De Witt, Iowa distribution)
John Kruper (age three and a half, placed with S. King and adopted)
Arthur Larson (age eight, placed with Warren Vanvactor)
Carl Larson (age five and a half)
Edwin Larson (age six)
Lucy Rapp (see Stanberry, Missouri distribution)
Alice Robinson-Johnson (replaced in Afton, Iowa with Dr. E. M. Johnson)
Clara Schmidt (age seven, placed with H. R. Wayman, Princeton, Missouri)
Charlotte Mabel White (placed with Mrs. John Whitmeyer of Chulu, Missouri)

Mr. Swan and Miss Hill were present. One woman was bound to have a girl I had there and when she went to another place this woman vowed she would make her trouble so the child would not stay. She did so and I had to take her into Iowa for placing.

Master Leo Burning was said to be a "Jap." I think he was the only Japanese child I ever had to place. He was a pretty boy, but was taken sick and was so patient. He had to be taken back to New York.

Beatrice Chadwick was born November 6th, 1898. She later moved to Kansas City, Missouri.

Isadore Ethel Doyle was born October 4th, 1897. James Doyle was born March 7th, 1898 or 1899. Their real parents had separated and their mother had married again to Emery Brezer of Cobbleskill, New York. Two other brothers are named Alfred and Howard. Alfred is at the House of Refuge, Randalls Island, New York.

John Kruper was born June 23rd, 1901.

The Larson brothers kept their homes. Arthur Larson was born April 20, 1902.

Alice Robinson was born May 1, 1898. She was replaced in Afton, Iowa and adopted. She married Don Linville on August 5th, 1910. They have one daughter. Alice was a fine pianist and a handsome girl. She has brothers Willie, Herbert and Henry.

In this company was Clara Schmidt from the Gallitin, Missouri party. She was placed a little later and was a pathetic case. When reaching the home where I was to leave her, she would not stay, but ran out and climbed into the carriage and I had to take her into the house again. Again she escaped and grabbed hold of the carriage wheel as I attempted to drive off. Again I took her in and starting away, she ran down the road following the liveryman and myself and crying, "Oh, Mr. Clarke, take me with you. I want to go with you." I stopped the horses and told the liveryman that I must go back and do it all over again. Getting out of the carriage, I approached her when suddenly she stopped, and holding her hands up said, "Go on Mr. Clarke." She ran back at once to her new home and was contented. A year or so later, when I had one lone girl to place in the community, that liveryman refused to go with me, saying he'd never go through that scene again. Clara was later taken to Nora Springs, Iowa and then West Branch where her brother Ernest was. She then went back to Wayman's and later to New York, where she became a nurse. She married in Bronx, New York.

Charlotte Mabel White was born January 16th, 1892. She was first placed in Missouri in 1901. She married Emanuel Dumler. She has a sister named Edith Maud White (Mrs. Virgil Wingate).

(next page). Company of children for the Princeton, Missouri distribution. Agents in back (left to right): H. D. Clarke, Anna Laura Hill and J. W. Swan. Children in back row (left to right): Bertha Beckman, Ethel Doyle, Alice Robinson, Clara Schmidt and Beatrice Chadwick. Children in center row (left to right): Arthur Larson, Edwin Larson, Lucy Rapp, James Doyle and Carl Larson. Front left: John Kruper. Front right: Leo Burning.

HOMES WANTED

For Children

A Company of Orphan Children of different ages in charge of agents will arrive at your town on date here in mentioned. The object of the coming of these children is to find homes in your midst, especially among farmers, where they may enjoy a happy and wholesome family life, where kind care, good example and moral training will fit them for a life of self-support and usefulness. They come under the auspices of the New York Children's Aid Society. They have been tested and found to be well-meaning boys and girls anxious for homes.

The conditions are that these children shall be properly clothed, treated as members of the family, given proper school advantages and remain in the family until they are eighteen years of age. At the expiration of the time specified it is hoped that arrange ments can be made whereby they may be able to remain in the family indefinitely. The Society retains the right to remove a child at any time for just cause, and agrees to re move any found unsatisfactory after being notified.

Remember the time and place. All are invited. Come out and hear the address. Applications may be made to any one of the following well known citizens, who have agreed to act as a local committee to aid the agent in securing homes.

L. B. WOODS, J. C. LOMAX, H. C. BOWSHER, T. S. BALLEW, E. R. CASTEEL, SCHUYLER KING, M. F. ROBINSON, EMMETT CLEMENTS.

The distribution will take place at

THE OPERA HOUSE, PRINCETON, MO.

Thursday, Jan. 18, at 10:30 a. m. and 2 p. m.

J. W. SWAN, H. D. CLARKE. **Agents**

Dodger for the Princeton, Missouri distribution of January 18, 1906.

Beatrice Chadwick.

Isadore and James Doyle, ages eleven and nine, respectively.

(top). John Kruper.

(bottom). Florence Kahnis.

(top left). Arthur Larson.

(top right). Alice Robinson.

(bottom). Charlotte Mabel White.

PLATTSBURG, MISSOURI - FEBRUARY 18th, 1906

Some children placed were:
Anna Brogden (age three)
Harold Brunner (age four)
Mabel Dickenson
William Doyle
Alfred Goegel
Emil Lods
Elizabeth McIntosh
Joseph Mitchel
Alice Robinson (replaced in Afton, Iowa with Dr. E. M. Johnson-see
  Princeton, Missouri distribution)
Henry Robinson
Bettie Watt

The local pastor, who offered prayer at our distribution, preached the next Sunday and told his congregation that there were sixty families in his parish without a child and as far as he knew, not one of them took a child of us.

Anna Brogden was from the Home for the Friendless. She went to Nebraska and had a brother Alfred at Afton, Iowa.

Harold Brunner was found on the city streets and never knew his name, only the one given to him by guess. He was about four years old. No relative was ever found.

William Doyle was abandoned by his father and his mother is dead.

Emil Lods had a sister I placed at Kirkman, Iowa. They were French. Nothing was known about parentage. The sister was later claimed by a relative and had to go, I believe.

Elizabeth McIntosh was Scotch. I have no history for her. She had a sister placed in Kansas City.

Joseph Mitchel came down with scatter fever and was taken to Chicago to an orphanage and then on to New York City.

Bettie Watt was Scotch. Her parents were living. She went to Nebraska, but was later returned to New York City.

Others went here and there, the distribution not resulting in placing all in that community.

HOPKINTON, IOWA - MARCH 15th, 1906

<u>Children placed were</u>:
Alfred Bauman (placed with Matt Pierce)
Kathleen Marie Belt
Amy Calhoun (placed with W. E. Doane)
William Faust
Bernice Lindergren (placed with E. M. Ferguson)
Gertrude Perry (placed with Samuel Orr)
Emily Reese (placed with Mr. and Mrs. C. U. Parker in Chicago,
  Illinois and replaced several times later)
Ira Rowland (placed with A. D. LeClere)
Joseph Rowland (placed with Ben Kurth)

Had Anna Laura Hill along as assistant. Alfred Bauman was born February 13th, 1903. He was one of the finest boys. He had been deserted by his parents or relatives. Matt Pierce took him and about worshipped him, as did his daughter Kittie. Alfred often wrote me after that, up until about 1913, when I heard nothing more.

I mention among the many, this one sad case: Kathleen Belt was destined to be a great sufferer. She was born September 29th, 1896. A young man in her first home disliked her and she was removed. The second home had no children and her faults were greatly magnified and told over and over at the tables in front of her and company at the house. I took her to Missouri. Here, she was bewitched and her foster parents did not know how to manage her and the poor thing had to go. All these homes had good references, but failed to keep her. I brought her to Minnesota. She would go to school with bleeding lips, or cheeks, or arm, or something and would tell that her foster mother did it when punishing her. At last she fell down stairs and broke her arm. The doctors declared the arm was not broken, but it became stiff at the elbow and her flesh as hard as a bone. I visited her and asked if she had been punished severely and she said "No." One cold winter evening the home burned down and she had to be taken to a neighbor. She was then returned to me again. Our Ladies Aid Society of the church clothed her up again and she stole a few

242

cents while they were doing it for her. She bought bananas with the money and treated the women before it was discovered. I took her to the New York City Hospital for treatment and then she was removed to another home. I visited her, finding her in a most pitiable condition. The poor child would weep for me to help her. At last she died of rheumatism about the heart. Why must a child suffer like that?

Amy Calhoun was born January 17th, 1898. She was a bright Irish girl and was taken by a jeweler, adopted, and well educated. I hear nothing from her now, but I always called on her when in that vicinity.

Bernice Lindergren was a baby of the party and a sweet one she was. She was born December 25th, 1905. She was adopted, but later on her foster mother died. The "grandmother" cared for her and her foster father and she has been in school doing well. She sends me an occasional word. She grew up to be a nice young lady.

Gertrude Perry was born September 24th, 1901. She was a bright and active child and was very small for her age. She had three homes before she was settled permanently. She was very nervous, but had promise. She liked music and was a pianist. She finally went to Lansing, Iowa up on the Mississippi Bluffs with Seventh Day Adventists and wrote me nice letters. She went to music school in Indiana. Relatives that were found at Albany, New York wanted me to give her money to visit them, but I refused, thinking I had to ask some questions regarding them first. This made her angry. She went and was never heard from again.

Enroute, a friend in Chicago named C. U. Parker had met us at the Union Station and picked out our oldest girl Emily Reese, and we let him have her, with her consent. Emily was born March 28th, 1892 in Brooklyn, New York. In a few months I had to replace her in Iowa. In this second home she was in peculiar circumstances and complaints were made that seemed unsatisfactory, but I removed her again. In the third home she was not well clothed and again I took her. In doing so, her foster brother, in a great wrath, made terrible threats that he thought was enough to put me in silence regarding her being neglected by them. Years later this young man had charge of a lighthouse in Florida and he wrote asking forgiveness for his rudeness, but wanted to know where his "only sister he ever had" was. This I declined to give, but I frankly forgave him. Next, she was placed with Seventh Day Adventists and united with their church. It was a good home and she was a good girl there, but they had a large family and were moving about and taking her to their camp meeting, left her there for me to come and get. I brought her into Wisconsin to another family of the same faith and later she was coaxed away from her home by a family of the same church and they urged her to go to South Dakota, where their people had a Sanitarium. Arriving there, she found that she was not old enough and had not enough education. She sent to me for help and I sent her money. She was studying to become a nurse. She wrote, "Do you think enough of me, Mr. Clarke, to help me once more?" I sent her five dollars to buy books with and she again started in school. She was soon urged to come back and marry a young man named Earl Kidder in Wisconsin, which she did on March 20th, 1912 in Janesville. They now reside on a farm near Edgerton, Wisconsin. There I have visited she and her husband twice since and she now has two pretty little children. She seemingly forgot all the help I gave her and for several years has refused to write to me.

Ira Rowland was born June 29th, 1900. Joseph Rowland was born February 17th, 1903. Ira went to a French family and Joseph to a German family. The German family had three daughters of peculiar makeup. One had black eyes and brown hair. The other had brown eyes and black hair and the third had pink eyes and white hair (albino).

(next page). Hopkinton, Iowa company. Agents in back are H. D. Clarke and Anna Laura Hill (holding Bernice Lindergren). Child in back: Kathleen Marie Belt. Center row (left to right): Alfred Bauman, Amy Calhoun, Joseph Rowland, Ira Rowland, Gertrude Perry. Child on front left: Samuel Orr. Emily Reese not in photo. Photo taken in Hopkinton, Iowa.

(top). Alfred Bauman

(bottom). Amy Calhoun.

Bernice Lindergren with foster parents.

Emily Reese "when of age."

Ira (r) and Joseph (l) Rowland.

AFTON, IOWA - APRIL 5th AND NOVEMBER 1st, 1906

Some children placed were:
Charles Blair
Alfred Brogden
Josephine Conner (placed with Albert Schwantz)
Irene Gunderson (placed in same home as her brother Thomas below)
Mamie "May" Gunderson (twin)-(placed in same home as above)
Thomas Gunderson (twin)-(placed in same home as above)
Thomas Hansen (replaced in Nebraska)
Henry Hanson
Harry Johnson
John Johnson
Myron McDonald
Lee Peterson
Edward Reck (placed with G. W. Kelley)
Alice Robinson-Johnson (placed with Dr. E. M. Johnson-see
  Princeton, Missouri distribution)
Herbert Robinson
Willis Robinson
Sarah Smalling
Valentine Smalling
Hazel Watts-Forgy (placed with R. J. Forgy)

    I had as usual, previously arranged for this distribution. The applications were so many that we took a second company in November. I had one boy that was placed with a wealthy farmer, but was not treated well and became very unhappy and ran away. He was then sent with Mr. Swan (a Society agent) to Nebraska, but enroute he was taken from the Creston, Iowa station by a friend of this farmer and rushed to the judge at Osceola, Iowa to be appointed guardian. I headed him off and defeated that. He hid the boy away and later he turned up farther north with a guardian appointed and the boy being contented, we let him stay without further disturbance. The other children did quite well.

Charles Blair was from Elmira, New York.

Had Alfred Brogden again, who had a nice sister in Nebraska.

Josephine Conner was adopted as Schwantz.

Irene Gunderson was the younger sister of Mamie and Thomas. She was born December 25th, 1895. One of the Gunderson girls was a twin to the brother. Irene stayed in her home until nearly of age when a disagreement between she and her foster mother caused a dismissal and they were not going to give her her clothes. I compelled them to give them to her for their own self respect and they did. She was very grateful to me. She was a very nice girl, but died on December 16th, 1918. She is buried in Afton, Iowa. May was born February 12th, 1893. Mamie married Joseph Shroyer November 28th, 1917 in Uniontown, Pennsylvania. She was a splendid girl. Thomas Gunderson served in the World War.

Harry and John Johnson went to Griswold, Iowa and did finely.

Lee Peterson went to Nebraska.

Edward Reck was born July 5th, 1897. He has a brother named "Wick."

Hazel Watts was born October 8th, 1898. Her mother, in dying, had signed a surrender to her pastor. The pastor gave her to the Aid Society to place out. We found her a good home on a farm near Afton, Iowa, but the surrender papers were not recorded before the mother's death and therefore were void. The unworthy father at once instituted proceedings to get her and sued for ten thousand dollars. When informed of this, I hastened with all speed and had the foster parents taken at once to the County Seat to adopt her. This defeated the father in some way. He had not taken care of her and the mother when she was living. The sad ending was that when nearly of age, the girl ran away and married. They took her and her husband back to their home and were kind to them. Later on she ran away from her husband and went east to some of her people.

HOMES WANTED

—FOR—

CHILDREN

A

Company of Orphan Children

of different ages in charge of an agent will arrive at your town on date herein mentioned. The object of the coming of these children is to find homes in your midst, especially among farmers, where they may enjoy a happy and wholesome family life, where kind care, good example and moral training will fit them for a life of self-support and usefulness. They come under the auspices of the New York Children's Aid Society. They have been tested and found to be well meaning boys and girls anxious for homes.

The conditions are that these children shall be properly clothed, treated as members of the family, given proper school advantages and remain in the family until they are eighteen years of age. At the expiration of the time specified it is hoped that arrangements can be made whereby they may be able to remain in the family indefinitely. The society retains the right to remove a child at any time for just cause, and agrees to remove any found unsatisfactory after being notified. Remember the time and place. All are invited. Come out and hear the address. Applications may be made to any one of the following well known citizens, who have agreed to act as local committee to aid the agent in securing homes.

N. W. ROWELL, H. F. SPURGEON, DR. J. W. LAUDER, L. W. McLENNAN, B. T. NIX, C. F. SANDER, G. L. BARNUM, A. T. BURROWS.

The Distribution Will Take Place

At the Opera House, Afton, Iowa, on Thursday, April 5, 1906,

At 1:30 p. m.

Office, 105 E. 22nd Street, New York City.

B. W. TICE and H. D. CLARKE, Agents

Dodger for the Afton, Iowa distribution of April 5, 1906.

(top). Josephine Conner.

(bottom). Irene (l) and May (r) Gunderson.

(top). Hazel Watts.

(bottom). Edward Reck at age eight.

WINNEBAGO, MINNESOTA - JANUARY 11th, 1907

Some children placed were:
Axel Erickson
Edna Hudson (age one year and nine months, placed with Ernest
  Snare)
Florence McGuire (age eleven)
Valentine O'Day (age eight and a half, placed with Mrs. Mary Johnson
  of Mapleton, Iowa)
Charles Watson (age ten, placed with William Hardtke)
Oswald G. Watson (age ten and nine months)
Anna Wexler (age eleven, placed with Abram Jacket)
George Wexler (age three, placed with Winfield Smith of Truman,
  Minnesota)
Lena Wexler (age thirteen, placed with George Andrews)
Sadie Wexler (age six, placed with George Oliver of Amboy,
  Minnesota)
Hugh Wilson (age ten)
Oswald Wilson
Catherine Zurn (age eleven)
Fred Zurn (placed later)
Rosa Zurn (age thirteen)

My wife went with me to New York after these children. While at Winnebago arranging for this distribution, the hotel keeper did not wish to keep us when we arrived. I assured him the children would be kept orderly and not drive patrons away, as he expected them to do. He consented and said afterward that he never saw as orderly and well behaved children in all his life.

We arrived the night before the distribution at the Opera House. My wife had full care of the seven girls and was complimented on her ability. One of the girls was a baby and she was placed far from town on a farm. Her name was Edna Hudson. She was born March 3rd, 1905. As soon as she could write she became a correspondent and this lasted until after her graduation from High School at seventeen years. She wanted to study to be nurse, but had already commenced keeping company with a young man. She married Herbert L. Velta on July 23rd, 1924 in Delevan, Minnesota.

All the children were placed quickly except Florence McGuire. This girl's mother had four children and was a rag picker on the city streets, unable to care for her children. She was obliged to sleep in a basement of some tenement with her baby. I was to have the two older brothers, but they had the measles and could not go then, but later went to Nebraska. Florence was dreadfully afraid of who she called an "old person" (anyone over forty years old). She was born May 18th, 1895 in New York City. I placed her, but she came back to the hotel to me and again she was found a home. She cried bitterly for her mother. I had to again place her and then again and no place could keep her. At last I took her to Wasioja, Minnesota to the home of a merchant, where she grew up splendidly and became a very dignified girl; a fine singer. She married George E. Yates, a soldier in town and on October 14th, 1925, while at Dodge Center visiting, she came motoring down to see me with her husband, her brother from Nebraska and his foster parents. They had come to Minnesota to visit Florence.

Valentine O'Day was an Irish boy, but was much loved. He was born March 27th, 1898.

The four Wexlers were Hebrews and were very smart children. The mother had died and the father ran a news stand in northern New York City. He had died suddenly from a rupture of a blood vessel. He was a Russian Jew that had escaped to avoid military duty. There were seven children in the family. I took these four. One brother had went into business in the City and a sister was at Flint, Michigan. Lena was the main help in her father's business and had to take the place of the mother in the family and helped the father with the great bundles of papers. She was born March 15th, 1894. She had an attack of eye trouble and I took her to Chicago and sent her to specialists in New York City and then met her in Chicago upon her return and brought her back to her fine home in Winnebago. Lena was a good girl and stayed until old enough to care for herself. I later unfortunately placed her with a man of wealth, but the same day I found he was a wine bibber in his home and I at once went and tactfully rushed her away. I gave her to a good family. Her foster father was later a candidate for Lieutenant Governor of Minnesota, but was defeated. Lena was very appreciative and many are the beautiful expressive letters she has written me. She was graduated from the High School and was a clerk in her foster father's store. She went to Flint, Michigan to teach on October 29th, 1918. She became a Methodist Christian.

Anna Wexler was born July 22nd, 1895. Anna became a Baptist, but she had trouble in her home from deceiving them. I was to replace her, but succeeded in keeping the place for her and as a result she became very angry with me and would never write me again. She was ashamed to have people know she was a Jew. I told her to be proud of it and never ashamed of it. She too went to Flint, Michigan in 1918 to teach.

George Wexler was born April 27th, 1903. He was very head strong and had a few placings. If his last foster parents had not been unusually patient, he never would have kept a home. He too went to Flint, Michigan in 1918 to visit the sister who had once visited Anna when I was with her to adjust some troubles in the home. At Flint they taught school, were in offices and earning salaries of seventy-five dollars a month.

Sadie Wexler was born April 3rd, 1900. She was placed three or four times and she was a special favorite of mine. She was also placed in a Baptist home. She wrote me many fine letters until I left the work and she was shut off from writing. She too went to Flint, but then went back to her New York brother and she writes me that she has once again embraced her Hebrew faith.

The Wilsons and Watsons had some troubles. Charles Watson was born January 12th, 1896. He was living in Breda, Iowa in 1915.

Rosa and Catherine Zurn were sisters and finally went to the same home. Their mother had recently died. I took Catherine from her first home to visit Rosa and the man, not a Christian, had heard them praying in Rosa's room as he walked down the hall, asking God to not let them be separated, and he said that then he could not refuse to take both. He was not a Christian man, in fact was something of a godless man, but respectable, and his wife was O.K. They made their mother some very pretty embroidered things, one of which was a pretty waist shirt. Catherine was a fine seamstress, though a little girl. She had taken a prize in sewing. They moved to Aberdeen, South Dakota, where I visited them. They moved back to Winnebago, but I soon lost track of them.

I had one boy full of mischief who delighted in plaguing others. I had to assure him of authority and he soon learned it, for I had only to point my finger where I wanted him to sit when he was in mischief and he went straight away.

(top). Thomas Gunderson

(bottom). Florence McGuire.

Charles Watson.

Anna (back left), Lena (back right), George (front left) and Sadie (front right) Wexler.

LA PLATA, MISSOURI - OCTOBER 10th, 1907

<u>Some children placed were</u>:
Louis Bonesteele
Sadie Brooks (replaced January 23rd, 1908 with W. E. and Mary
  Sanders of Olewein, Iowa-see Hamilton, Missouri distribution)
Cecil Davis
Ernest Finger
Floyd Finger
Edward McCarty (age six)
Marguerite McCarty (age seven)
Grace Milburn
Daniel Paine
Isaac L. Rose
Raymond Rose
Albert Schad
Carl Schad (placed with A. R. Kelson of Sioux City, Iowa)

With me here was the nurse, Miss Hill and Kansas agent, W. W. Bugbee. It was a very interesting company and successful distribution.

Louis Bonesteele was taken in to Kansas by Mr. Bugbee.

Cecil Davis was deserted by parents and later returned to New York City.

Ernest and Floyd Finger were nice brothers. They went to Greencastle and were adopted by the same family. They were happy correspondents for a time. I love to think of all such wards and their loving words later on.

Marguerite and Edward McCarty went to one home in Ethel, Missouri and later seemed to change their names, as though in another home. Their address was then in Waukenda, Missouri, RD # 2. This was not explained. Marguerite went to California, but came back and was replaced and then had to go out and care for herself. She became a nurse. She often wrote to me, but died rather mysteriously and no particulars were given to me. She was considered a very fine young woman.

Grace Milburn was taken at Ethel, Missouri and later married a Mr. Pritchard, a farmer. I get nice letters from her occasionally. She married happily from her accounts.

Daniel Paine went to Kirkville, Missouri and was adopted. He was also a deserted child.

Raymond Rose went to Kansas with Bugbee.

Albert Schad drifted about and when of age went to Detroit, rather dissipated. Albert moved to Arkansas and Texas and had a large family of girls.

Carl Schad was born March 28th, 1903. He was four years old and was taken by a Kelson family on being replaced and was later adopted. He was wild, but they clung to him affectionately. After he went away, he seemed to look back with appreciation on the home that he had received. He now writes nice little letters. The Kelsons were a fine family of Seventh Day Adventists. Carl went to Detroit, married a Canadian girl and works for the Ford Auto Company. He owns his own home and has three children. I visited them in the Autumn of 1926 and took their pictures. I get very interesting letters from Mabel Kelson, the older daughter.

Some brothers and sisters in these La Plata wards were separated far apart. While pathetic, it seemed to be for the best, and in years to come, they would meet again or come into communication with each other.

These children from New York and other cities that were placed on farms seemed mostly cured of their physical and mental faults. Accustomed to the excitements of the city, the life in the country and open air and their activity, had a great tendency to call their minds away from former evils that exist in the crowded tenements. The farm, more than anything else, is a "Seminary of Industry, teaching order and common sense and self reliance." I could place girls in better homes in towns with better results than boys. Indeed, few men in towns ever wanted to take a boy to raise there. There seems to be a general opinion that it is dangerous as a rule.

Village life is dangerous because of the great lack of religious integrity of men in general and the commercial spirit that dominates business men. They do not educate by precept and example the children in virtue, honesty and Christianity. The farmer is hardly more religious than his town brother, but the farm has its open air and other health giving activities and freedom from city temptations, a great advantage for the boy.

(Authors Note): Reverend Mr. Clarke wrote the following article for an unknown publication regarding the above distribution:

Twelve O.K.'D - Thirteenth Unlucky

Two days and two nights as usual on the train from New York City to the great and powerful West. "Are we going out west," said little Isaac. "Out West" is a magic word for the homeless city boy or girl. Even after reaching Missouri and having breakfast and resting the tired little waifs, we were asked if we were "out West." "Yes, this is the West," we assured them and the anticipation was still greater. "I'm hungry for love and a home." "Now we are going to have a papa," said one who was going to have a great meeting. "You must keep just as still while I talk and then you will have new homes," I said as we headed for the Opera House. Crowds were in the streets to see us march and all kinds of curious remarks could be heard. "My, aren't that a sweet little fellow," "There's the boy I want." "Poor little fellow," and all such remarks. The Opera House was crowded and standing room "at a premium" as they say. Some had come twenty-five miles to get a boy or girl and had to return disappointed, though one family was well rewarded for the long drive that morning. The Professor of the Public School said that one hundred families had sent requests that their children be permitted to be absent from classes to go and see the orphans, so he dismissed the whole school for a half-hour and I gave them a short special talk on their great privileges in contrast with the thousands of poor in the great cities.

In a semicircle the children sat on the "stage" and the crowd in front sat an hour and a half at the first meeting to hear the address and watch the children. A good revivalist could then and there have "started a revival," for the text was a living one and the people were very tender in feeling and thought.

The usual speech or talk ended, now the children must be introduced. One by one they stepped forth in front of their seat, to be the object of great curiosity and special interest to some certain ones who perhaps wanted a child. It did not seem to embarrass the little folks as they hardly seemed to realize the object in view. If it were not for the good results following, this public exhibition would seem quite out of place.

Here is Ramond, aged eight years, and his brother Isaac, nice boys, surrendered to the Society by their father. He may never see them again. Why does he give two such pretty and healthy children away? You tell or guess. The boys are separated and go to homes about ten miles apart. It is awful, but a necessity. Necessities are awful things. Lewis B. - nine years old; black hair, pretty eyes, large of age and healthy. He has no relatives from whom to be separated. He was taken by a man from Kansas visiting in the town and the Kansas agent will look after his interests from year to year. Daniel P. - seems to be the favorite in the crowd of applicants, for he gets more applications than the other boys. A nice woman in the next town north is on hand offering a good home for him. Her husband is a carpenter and the State Normal School is just across the road. Daniel was deserted by his relatives, and his mother has not been seen in nearly two years. Dear reader, do you know what it is to be deserted in childhood and in innocence? But what sayeth the Scripture? "When my father and my mother forsake me, then the Lord will take me up." Is this the way he does it? Sadie B. - is a pretty girl of eight years. She, too, was abandoned by her mother who has not been seen in three and one-half years. She is a very modest but affectionate girl. A mail carrier has taken her and a nice home with no children now has sunshine. A home without a child is about, or less than, half a home. Carl and Albert S .- are brothers, four and a half and eleven years; one with light hair and the other black hair. One awful day a father and mother quarreled and parted and the father surrendered the boys. Did you ever see or hear a family quarrel? What awful things people do when they are angry. These nice boys went to one home without separation. Edward and Marguerite, brother and sister, aged six and seven years, pretty children and inseparable. Mother incompetent to care for them. They, too, are placed in one home and are happy. Ernest and Floyd are another pair of brothers and go to one home. A man and wife came twenty miles to find a boy and girl. He is superintendent of a Methodist Sunday School and owns 360 acres of land and had no children. There are hundreds of thousands of homes with no children, in this country, and so many that do not want any. It might keep some ladies "out of society," you know. And now we have Grace W. - , a sweet girl of nearly eight years. She has been three years in the Orphan Asylum. On the train with a tablet and pencil she displayed some talent as an artist. A nice home that years ago adopted one of our boys wanted Grace and so she goes to grace the home and bring the grace of God to loving hearts that shelter the homeless. That makes twelve placed. There is another, the thirteenth, Cecil D - , eight years; very affectionate but diseased eyes and other defects. He, too, was deserted by his parents. He was very needy indeed and it would have been a great charity to have taken him and given him loving care, but nobody wanted to do as much as that. Then, again, it was not "policy," as the learned say, to bring such a boy with others or to place such in homes in "the West," and the law, too, is against it; so he was sent back to New York City. How the poor boy did love me and seek care. But back he went. He will be well cared for but not in a real home. He will have no new papa and mamma or foster sister.

And now we leave them all to grow in the affections of those who have taken them and grow up virtuous and self-reliant and some day take their part in the great activities of life. We hope they will all have:
Fireside enjoyments,
And all the comforts of the lowly roof.

(top). Sadie Brooks.

(bottom). Carl Schad.

BLAIR, NEBRASKA - (DATE UNKNOWN)

Some children placed were:

Ida Elizabeth Cook (placed with William Slonecker of Tamora, Nebraska and replaced April 28th, 1904 with Mrs. Martha (George) Spurlock of Schuyler, Nebraska)

Rosa Moyan (placed November 7th, 1903 at Greenwood, Nebraska and replaced December 25th, 1903 to Tamora, Nebraska-see also Osceola, Iowa distribution)

Lizzie Palm

This was the same as other distributions. One girl of the Blair company was Lizzie Palm. She had black curly hair and black eyes and a dark complexion. She was placed with a hardware merchant, but had to be removed. I took her to Coon Rapids, Iowa and later to Castana, Iowa and from there she went to Rodney, Iowa to a maiden lady, a so-called Christian Science in faith. She asked if her religion prevented her from having the child. As we can not place all the children in the exact homes we best like, we made no distinction between denominations, only that they teach virtue, industry, clothe them well and send them to the public school, as well as an organized church and Sunday School. This she promised to do, but did not. She simply went over to her brother's house to have some "readings" and called that going to church. I called her attention to her breach of contract. Later on she asked the privilege of giving the girl to her sister at Ute, Iowa, who was in a hotel. I refused the request. Secretly, she placed her there and with misrepresentations had her adopted by the hotel family. She then snapped her fingers in my face and said, "You've nothing more to say about it." I mention this as a case where a Christian Scientist can tell a falsehood in a county court and feel all right about it. In a few days I went quietly to the court to satisfy myself that adoption had taken place and then engaged a lawyer and secured a writ of habeas corpus from Judge Mould. I thought I would serve the writ myself and save the Sheriff's fees, but finally concluded to let the sheriff do it. I secured an order from the Judge to let me see the girl alone. They refused me, but on presentation of the order said I could see her ten minutes. I said that was all I wanted.

I told Lizzie the situation and that the adoption was contested and that she would be brought into court, but not to fear, for I was her friend. I was greatly abused by the family and soon left. At the trial I found that the Sheriff, the Postmaster, the editor of the local paper, the station agent - ten in all, were against me.

The trial took place at the Courthouse at Sioux City, Iowa on the sixth day of May 1907. David Mould was District Judge. The case was in law #4424, docket 26, page 224. The defendants had the County Attorney for a lawyer. It seems he had been their helper all along in the unlawful proceedings. It was a hard fought case, taking nearly all day, and I was alone in the prosecution.

I had made it the subject of much earnest prayer that God would rule for the best. I contended that a hotel had been disgraced, but I did not bring it into the testimony. I showed that the Children's Aid Society was the legal guardian of the child and I it's agent. I showed that the course of the foster parent was a breach of her contract with me and I had a better place for her.

The defendant tried to show that the hotel in question was above the average and that I could do no better with the girl and I had already placed her in three homes. The papers had already had articles dictated by their friends and the Ute paper had a most insulting article and said that when the trial was over that H. D. Clarke, the agent, would have no more say about Lizzie Palm. The city dailies came out with statements of the trial and spoke of the beauty of the girl and false statements, such as that my attorney and myself had called on the girl privately, trying to get the girl to leave her home and come with me. The agent of the Iowa State Home had written a private letter to the Judge, pleading this case as a "precedent" and not to leave the orphanages without authority in such cases, for then any one in like circumstances would have it easy to adopt a child against the consent of the Home that had sheltered the child cared for and placed.

The judge ruled that he would not take the child away from the Society, but he expressed the wish that the contending parties might enter into some new agreement. Wisely or unwisely, I consented and drew up a new contract, whereby they could not give or take the child to any place without my consent, not to any hotel except on a brief visit, with the foster parent with her. And so the girl went back to the former home where I had placed her. The adoption was set aside by the Judge on June 5th, 1907. Though I won the case, I was much chagrined over the results. I had desired to cut loose entirely from the family and take the girl far away.

In December, when I made the annual visit there, I was refused an interview with the girl. They had already broken their contract, leaving the girl at the hotel for three months while away on a visit. I visited the girl at the schoolhouse and revealed to her what she did not know before, that she had five brothers and two sisters living elsewhere. This terribly angered the family. This was my last visit with the girl. She was about twelve years of age at the time of the suit. On general principles, I would never place a child with a so-called Christian Scientist again. It was neither Christian or Science. I once again heard from the girl.

While on the whole, this orphan work was very fascinating, yet these and other incidents show fearful perplexities and burdens.

There are too many to record here. My correspondence has been very interesting and profitable and encouraging to the wards, who seem to love me and write so appreciatively. They are scattered all over the United States, from Atlantic to Pacific. My correspondence with these children has probably averaged from eight hundred to two thousand letters a year. The past two years (1926, 1927 to May 1928) has seen an average of two letters a day, every day in the year. Some wards have become destitute and appeal to me for aid. The vast majority have grown up what the world calls respectable citizens. Some are active Christian workers. Some are Christians in the ministry.

Some dear friends say it was the greatest work of my life. The God of the Orphan is the judge of that. The work is in God's hands. He will know what may be a failure and what a success. God grant I may in the world eternal meet many of them redeemed, and never again homeless.

Ida Elizabeth Cook.

MISCELLANEOUS PLACINGS

There were very many other distributions by myself and Mr. Tice in the northwest. I have placed children in every state from New York to Nebraska and Minnesota to Texas. In 1910 I made an extensive trip into Nebraska, visiting wards in the northern part of the state, many in the sand hills. One house visited was a sod house. There were also many single placings and I will give a few below:

EMMA C. - She was a German, her father coming to this country. He was a brass finisher. The mother died. I placed her with the president of a bank. His own daughter made trouble and Emma had to go. I then placed her with a German family where she was "confirmed." She sent me her confirmation picture. She was a fine girl, but became afflicted with "St. Vitas Dance" and I sent her to New York for treatment, where she was cured. An aunt in New Jersey sent for her. The father had tried again and would not keep his own child. She wrote many nice letters after her cure, but I soon lost all track of her.

ANGELINA, PHILOMENA AND MARIE DEL VECCHIO - These three Italian girls were born at Naples, Italy. They were first placed in Missouri in 1905. I took them from Paris, Missouri in 1907. Their mother was dead. Their father was Domico Del Vecchio and was a day laborer. Marie went to the Houch family north of Corning, Iowa, on a farm. At one time she was very sick at the Public Hospital at Cresco, Iowa, where I visited her. She was a faithful and very useful girl. In 1927 she was in South Dakota at work, still unmarried and in the best of health. Angelina "Anna" went to Murray, Iowa first on a farm where they worked her fearfully hard. I had a time in removing her to Corning, near her sister Marie. She was averse to restraint, but got along without trouble. She married very unhappily and the man later died. She married a Mr. Wilcox and lives at Blanchard, Iowa. She has four children from both marriages.

Philomena "Phila" went to Denton, Montana with her folks. She was a very bright and active "happy-go-lucky" girl. She married one Frank Rowbotham and lived at Arlington, South Dakota in 1927. She has three boys and two girls.

Left to right: Marie, Philomena and Angelina Del Vecchio.

GEORGE AND PEARL GAIDE - Pearle was adopted and married well. George graduated at High School, at College and studied for the Methodist ministry. He is pastor of the East Dubuque Methodist Church and has two children. I visited him in December 1925 and spoke in his church.

George and Pearl Gaide.

ANDREW M. - In October of 1910, I had a strenuous case at Ord, Nebraska. Andrew M. ran away from his home, representing that he was misused. He found an evil advisor who wanted to be appointed guardian. I went to the boy and found that he was very unreliable. I went to the man who wanted to be guardian and explained all the responsibilities he would have to assume, the expense and troubles. When he saw what it all meant to him, he declined. The judge however, would not allow me to take Andrew out of state under existing laws, but I had quietly done so without seeing the judge. All would have blown over, however, I left the boy and the judge promised not to appoint any other guardian, and to do the right thing with the boy. I do not think he ever amounted to much and probably drifted about.

HARRY MCKENZIE - Harry McKenzie was born April 14th, 1893. He was educated at Highland Park College in mechanical and electrical departments. He became an electrician and garage worker in 1913 with the Johnston Motor Company in Des Moines, Iowa. Harry was placed on a farm at Griswold, Iowa. He was Scotch. He was a bashful boy of eleven years, very industrious. His mother died when he was seven. Her name was Eliza Clark, which interested me. In 1909 his foster father moved to town, but did not want to take the boy there. He wanted to leave him on the farm with the man who rented it, but without wages. Harry was now sixteen. I would not let him remain just for clothes and board, for he was an industrious boy. I hired him out at Kirkman, Iowa for ten dollars a month and he did nicely. He went to school in the winter. He was a very bashful boy, but the pretty teacher was crippled and Harry wheeled the chair for her, having won her confidence, or she his. She seemed to have much influence over him. He was a very independent boy. The next year his wages were increased until I had two hundred dollars saved for him in the bank. He entrusted his wages to me for safe keeping. He wanted to buy a motor cycle for one hundred dollars. At first I hesitated. He had never ran one, but was a natural mechanic. I consented. He used it a year and sold it for thirty dollars. He was a chauffeur for a while. I lost track of him after a long correspondence.

FLORENCE MURPHY - She was placed previously by another agent. I placed her at Traer, Iowa with a blacksmith. She wanted to attend church one Sunday evening and her foster mother said "No." She then asked the man and he said "Yes." The family quarreled over it and sent for me. The man said, "If you take the girl away I'll leave my wife." The woman said, "If you leave the girl here I'll leave my husband." I shamed them out of that. I said to them, "You keep the girl a month and she is to obey whichever of you tell her first and the other is to keep still. At the end of the month, write me what you decide upon." In six weeks I got this from the man, "Come and get the girl. I have concluded to let my wife be the boss."

I took her away and replaced her. She was about fifteen years old at the time. She grew up, went back to New York City and became a nurse. I visited her there. When about of age, she wrote that she was about to be married. She had been ill and asked me for ten dollars to pay the doctor's bill and I sent it. She promised to pay it back, but never did. She had had trouble with her head. Two years later I heard from her that she and her husband had divorced. Still later I heard from her that she was again to be married. Last heard at this date (1928), she is in Florida.

THE RANDOLPHS - These were at Clarksville, Iowa. The father gave them up so he could marry again. He had five more children by the second wife. The oldest boy was turned away to the County House because he came down with tuberculosis. I visited him and gave him a bible and talked with him. He died happy in Jesus. The youngest sister also died. The remaining brother married and became a farmer, but having a large family, he had a hard time. Maggie was with an artist. She grew up well and married a printer. Elsie had a hard time in her home and was made to work and slave and ran away but half clothed. She tried to commit suicide and was a nervous wreck when I came to her. I placed her again where she was happy. She grew up and married a farmer and has a happy family.

(top). Elsie Randolph.

(bottom). Maggie Randolph.

FOUR STAUBER BOYS - These were all Hungarians. I placed them all in Minnesota. Their mother later came to see them and was pleased at my efforts for them. One of the boys was named Joseph.

Joseph Stauber (back right) with his foster family.

MINNIE U. - I have perhaps written about many of the worst cases, but they were few compared to the many good ones. One very sad case was Minnie U. in Missouri. She had a sad time of it in some homes and it was not always her fault. At last I placed her with a young man and wife who wanted her, but his father strongly protested against it and said his son was not fit to have a girl in the family. The young man's wife protested though, saying that it was all right, and insisted on taking the girl. I thought that if the wife could trust her husband with a girl in her family that it would be all right. Later on the husband and wife quarreled over the girl and he shot his wife, but did not kill her. He was arrested and sent to prison. The girl was taken away. I know not where the next agent took her.

I must leave unrecorded the vast majority of these children and youth, as interesting as they are. I may now as briefly as I can, and with interest, record the taking of some as wards of my own, as their guardian:

GUARDIANSHIPS

EFFIE MAY BENNETT - Effie was born March 9th, 1893. Her mother, whom I found years later, was Mrs. Henrietta Bennett, of Lake George, New York. I had placed Effie in several homes unsuccessfully in Iowa. She was one in our Osceola, Iowa company in 1904 (October twentieth). I then brought her into Minnesota, where she was kindly received by a Mrs. J., but the foster father and foster brother did not give her welcome. In a few years she was of age to leave and having developed an irresponsible habit of running away, it became necessary to place her in some institution for treatment and cure. While I was not legally appointed her guardian, she so regarded me and the institution also did. They looked to me for payment of the necessary fees, but Mr. Brace of New York City paid them. I took her to the State Home for such on May 16th, 1911. I often visited her, sent her money, books and little keepsakes and corresponded constantly. I located her brother, Herman Bennett, in Texas, who enlisted in the war and died. He left ten thousand dollars for his mother, who had turned him out of her home years before. I tried to get a share of this for Effie May and the War Department also made effort for me, but it could not be done. The mother still refused to take Effie. At last Effie's brother, R. T. Patrick of Warrensburg, New York arranged to have me send her to her mother at Lake George. I went after her and brought her to Battle Creek, Michigan in 1920 and then sent her on to her mother, where at this date she still is, but working out. I had looked after her for sixteen years.

EMMA JOAN CLARKE - Emma was born in New York City on September 22nd, 1905. Her father was H. B. Orkin, a wealthy merchant in that city and a Hebrew (German Jew). Her mother was Emma Barnard, from Montreal, Canada, a French Catholic whose family was prominent in Dominion affairs at one time. Emma Barnard worked for Mr. Orkin, a millionaire. Mr. Orkin deserted his child while she was a baby. Then the mother married another man named John Obell, Jr., and had a child named Clarice, when Emma was about three years of age. Mr. and Mrs. Obell, Jr. boarded Emma and then moved with Clarice to Cincinnati, Ohio. Mr. Obell was a candy maker in New York City until he moved to Cincinnati, when he became a collector for the David C. Cook Sunday School Supplies.

One Maurice Simons, a Frenchman and Catholic boarded Emma and on failure of the Obells to pay her board on time, he "spirited the child away," declaring they should never see her again.

When I was in Cincinnati with the Children's Home in 1912, I received word from the New York City Commissioner to try and look up Mrs. Obell. Evidently she had been trying through New York City authorities to find Emma. I was to find Mrs. Obell and report what I could find about her. That was a difficult job, as I had never heard of her before or knew where she was. I commenced the search and in a few weeks I located them on Garfield Avenue, opposite of where I roomed. It was a very roundabout way of finding the parties. First, I found Mr. Obell's father and mother. Then Obell Jr., Mrs. Obell giving me the particulars of the stealing away of her child. I promised her I would find Emma and free of charge, and for her to let the lawyers alone. Off and on I spent five months trying to locate Emma in New York City, among six million people. At last I succeeded in finding her at the Five Points, lower New York. After some bluffing and hard work I succeeded in getting the child and delivered her to her mother. Emma of course did not know her mother after being three years from her up and six years of age then. The child wanted to come and live with me. I often called on the family at various flats where they moved from time to time. I have her picture cards and candy.

One Sabbath morning on my way to the Jewish Temple where I occasionally went to services to hear the best singing in the city, I called on Mr. and Mrs. Obell at 904 Vine Street, Cincinnati. Emma was then seven years of age. Mr. Obell was having Clarice dressed for him to take to see the child's grandpa out in the suburbs of the city. Why did the Grandpa not come there to see her? He was deceiving his wife in order to run away with Clarice and desert Emma and her mother. I was at once suspicious. I said to them, "Mr. Obell, if you or your wife even happen to have to give up Emma, let me have her. You shall always know where she is and can correspond with or visit her if you wish." They thanked me and I left.

The next Wednesday I was in the country and received a letter from Mrs. Obell saying that her husband had deserted her and Emma and taken the baby Clarice with him, and that she had not a relative in the United States and but one friend, and that was me. I went to see her and found she had taken a small room and had but about thirty dollars left and no home or work.

We located Mr. Obell by means of his shipping a piano to his sister at Los Angeles. He had represented to his wife that his father lived at Denver, Colorado. She said if she could get to him there would be a chance to live with him and have her baby. The Chief of Police at Cincinnati offered to have him arrested and brought back, but it would cost her three hundred dollars, which would be refunded if he were convicted. She said she did not want him arrested, as they had lived peaceably together and that it was his mother who had gotten him away from her. Then through the Cincinnati Commissioner of Charities I secured a ticket for her to go to Los Angeles to be with him and she went and lived with him and Clarice nine years. Clarice died and she then gave Emma to me and signed the surrender papers on January 27th, 1913. She then became my child, though not through any judge or with legal adoption papers.

On January 29th, I started with Emma for Chicago, having with me an orphan girl named Clara Dearth to place at Bloomington, Illinois. Enroute on January 30th, I placed Emma in charge of the conductor on the C. N. W. Railway and sent her to Dodge Center and boarded her temporarily with Mrs. Clarence Tainter, a very fine woman. I paid her board there until such arrangements as I might make. Mrs. Obell did not go to California until March 18th, 1913.

In June 1913, cousin Dwight Clarke of Milton, Wisconsin thought he would like to have Emma live with them, and so I sent her there in company with daughter Florence. There seemed to be a little conflict between Dwight's boy and Emma and so at their request I removed her. C. J. and Jennie Burdick Carpenter wanted her and on October 11th, 1913 I sent her with Mrs. Mack to New Auburn, Minnesota.

On my retiring in Battle Creek, Michigan I went on an extended vacation east and April 22nd-27th, 1914 I went to visit Emma at New Auburn. She was delighted to see me and had about come to the conclusion that she was to live with the Carpenters. In the fall of that year, Mr. Carpenter made application to adopt Emma and I made a contract that I thought would make honorable my promise to Emma's mother, but they refused to sign it. I drew up five contracts and none of them would they sign. My last was the stipulation in regard to the mother's correspondence, etc. with Emma and that I was to be privileged to come and see her for a few days once in two years, and the alternate years she was to come at my cost and stay with me a few days. This was refused. In the meantime Emma's mother wrote me, pleading that I do not give Emma away. I sent for Mrs. Carpenter to bring Emma down to me at my expense at Dodge Center and I'd further communicate with the mother. She came with Emma on September 24th, 1914 expecting of course to take her back with her, but they had refused to sign the contract and I would not let the child return. This made such hard feelings on their part. They were fine people and would have given Emma a good home had they only agreed to my easy stipulations. I did not feel right about giving the child away when I had made the promise I did to her mother. I had rescued her from a stolen condition and was greatly attached to her in consequence. Hence she remained with me after that.

It has been a tragic life such as few girls could have stood and lived through safely. Will anyone blame me for my love and care of the stolen and castaway child? Her letters almost every week are of a literary style that few of her age can write. She is a great reader of Shakespeare, Browning, Kipling, Stevenson and others of great note. What the future will be, God only knows.

Reverend H. D. Clarke and Emma Joan Clarke. Photo was taken in Ohio.

ELIZABETH HICKEY-HENDERSON - Elizabeth had been placed on February 12th, 1903 with a Mr. and Mrs. Henderson of Corydon, Iowa and legally adopted. Her mother was Maggie Hickey from Rutland, Vermont. When but a baby, the mother was obliged to give up the girl. Mr. and Mrs. Henderson both died soon after taking her and left her twenty-two hundred dollars placed out on mortgage, but left her homeless. A kind lawyer at Corydon kept her a few weeks until I appeared on the scene. Elizabeth was born July 15th, 1894.

The attorney and the county judge appointed me legal guardian at Elizabeth's request. I agreed, giving bonds signed by Lou Van Horn of Garwin, Iowa. Elizabeth had quite a few household things that they left for her. These were stored for future use. I used the interest on her money to clothe her and such things as might be given her for comfort. I took her to Grinnell, Iowa where she was to work for her board and attend school. Soon, I replaced her with a Mr. and Mrs. Rivers of that city, and they were very kind and good to her. But again, I had to replace her, this time at Des Moines, Iowa. The home appeared to be first class, but it soon developed that the "mistress" was a very exacting arbitrary woman and gave the girl but very little time for school work. We had some controversy about it, but the girl was so afraid that she did not leave when I wanted her to, but in time the break came and she went to Jacks, a lawyer in Des Moines, with a very kind family. Here she finished High School and entered Business College. She later became a typist and stenographer for the Grinnell Car Company. She then married Mark DaShiell and put her money with his in a pretty home. Mark Jr. came to make the home happy.

In the meantime, about 1914, I had found her mother at Newark, New York and visited her and revealed to her the situation of her daughter. She was overjoyed. I acquainted Elizabeth of this and she was about wild to go out to see her mother, but circumstances hindered her and later she declared she did not want to go or have the mother come to her. Her pride and health, which was poor, caused this change of mind. She was a very fine girl and makes a very faithful affectionate wife and mother. Our correspondence is very pleasant and she looks to me as her dearest friend in days of need. She wrote these words to me on December 14th, 1913:

"My Dear Guardian,

I am pleased to know that you are to have a little vacation. I wish it was so you could run in and see my mother and report to me her condition. I hope she lives so I can sometime come and see her, for I am trying to save money enough to take an eastern trip. I am afraid I would collapse if I saw her, my poor unknown mother. Many a heartache have I had over wishing it were possible for me to help her, but I guess it is too late. Perhaps, if she had had a few rays of sunshine in early life, and about the time I was born, things would not be as they are. I only trust that God has forgiven my father, whether dead or alive. I never want to see him."

After I had seen the mother she wrote how thankful she was and almost wanted to come at once to see her mother. She said she would if she had ready money. She wanted me to get her a blue suit in the cities. She wrote after that she was having trouble with that Des Moines woman:

"You don't know what a comfort you have been to me the past year. I am so anxious to hear from you, but what shall I do? If I had had the money I might have taken a train. Really, she has been inhuman. Will you send me a five for fear I shall have to move my things real quick? Thank heaven I have a friend I can write my troubles to. If I only had a home of my own. I feel crushed and heartbroken. I feel that the Lord has done much for me and so have you. Please forgive me for what I have done in the past and may I be able to carry out my ambitions."

The poor girl, she was going to leave and was having a great struggle. The poor girl had been very cool and hardly been friendly when I had visited her in her distress with that woman, for fear if she did, she'd be turned into the street. She did not know how she could get away and not have a fight. She did it however, and the rage of that family was great. I received some very abusive letters from them.

I received a letter from her in November of 1914:

"Dear Guardian,

I have neglected you because I am busy and am to be married the twenty-fifth of this month. My name will be Mrs. Mark Dashiell. He is in business here. I will write particulars later."

Since her marriage and settlement in her own home, she writes gratefully of the past and wants me to come and see them and stay "as long as I wish." This guardianship was with much responsibility, but I do not regret it. I visited her and her husband in April of 1915. They had a child, Mark, Jr. and lived at 2517 East Lyon St., Des Moines, Iowa.

EDNA McKIBBEN (BEULAH VAN der SHURR) - Edna was born in the city of Cedar Rapids, Iowa on October 30th, 1900. Her mother was Elsie McKibben. When the babe was about five or six months of age, she gave the child to Reverend M. J. Van der Shurr of Kenwood Park, Iowa. She was legally adopted and took the name Beulah. Hence, I had known her since she was a babe. I frequently visited Mr. Van der Shurr, as he had dreams of establishing an orphanage, but lacked the financial ability and other qualifications. The child would come to my lap, hungry for affection and fondling. When she was about four and a half years of age, I happened to be there and said to Mr. Van der Shurr, "Give me this girl and I'll care for her, you have all you can support." "All right," he said. "Take her." That was all the contract I had. I at once took her with me to Welton, Iowa and secured a Mr. and Mrs. Forsythe to care for her. I assisted and paid for her music. She studied piano and violin. She was a very affectionate child and loved me dearly. I went as often as I could to see her. I took her in September of 1905.

In November of that year I brought her to Dodge Center, Minnesota to Reverend W. H. Ernst's, but they had taken a girl from another source and concluded not to assume the care of Beulah. At a church dinner a the Y.M.C.A. Hall she was asked to "speak a piece," though but five years of age. I placed her on a chair and for several minutes she rambled off an impromptu talk that at first we thought was something she had learned, but soon found it was "made up for the occasion" and I had to take her down.

On December 11th, 1905 I took her back to Welton. She stayed there up to September of 1916. She calls me "Grandpa Clarke." Mr. and Mrs. Forsythe did a great deal for her. I wanted to keep the child in my own home but my wife's health would not permit bearing the burden. The Forsythe's lost a girl at Milton College and Beulah was all the more welcome. In the summer of 1916 there was a misunderstanding between Beulah and the family and the neighbors that resulted in my letting her go to Milton, Wisconsin to attend High School, staying with G. R. Ross and family. I can never be able to repay all these good people for their great kindness to the girl. Time will somewhat heal their sorrows over the matter.

Upon going to Milton she wished to take the name Edna McKibben. Edna being the name her mother gave her. I would have been glad to have had her taken the name Clarke, as I was her guardian. Later she went back to Welton, Iowa where she graduated in High School and then taught school. Being of age now, she secured a place at Milton, Wisconsin and entered Milton College in the autumn of 1921. She married H. E. Barnes of Milton in 1924 and moved to Riverside, California in 1925.

Beulah Van der Shurr.

MARIE RICKS - BURDICK - DESIMPLE - INGLIS - In March or April of 1915, while on a mission among the Lone Sabbath Keepers in several states, I had stopped off at Marion, Iowa. I preached in The Church of God. After one service, I saw a German woman in the audience with a baby and I asked her in a joke if she had a baby to give away! In about three months I received a letter from her husband, Charles Burdick, asking me if I would take and place the baby in some home. I was much surprised, but after correspondence I found that the child was not his and that it must go to an orphanage if I did not take her. She was a very large child of her age. The father was one Julian Desimple, a Belgian. On August 17th, 1915 at five a.m. I took the baby to place somewhere and they were not to know where I secured her. Later at the General Conference, a woman from Marion saw the child and knew her and "let the cat out of the bag" to the chagrin of us all. The child was kept however and named Mary Louise. The own mother was Miss Hattie Ruth Rick of Faribault, Minnesota or near there. She herself was an orphan placed in an orphanage and later in a home at Waterville, Minnesota.

Distributions

FRANCES SCHROEDER - Frances was born April 16th, 1898 to German parents. She had two sisters that I placed at or near Plainview, Minnesota. This is where Frances was placed. Her sisters later married in California and at this writing live there. They were adopted by a Mr. and Mrs. Knapp. Frances was a useful girl, good looking and well meaning. She was a little frail in health at first. Her foster mother, while loving the girl greatly, was jealous of the regard her husband had for Frances after they had had a baby of their own and the girl, agreeing that it was best, asked me to remove her. The foster mother continued to be a good friend and made her many useful presents. I brought her to Pleasant Corners and when she was beyond common school, I placed her at Kasson for a High School education. There was some danger of her being taken away on account of doubts of her staying in a home, and lest she be disturbed in her studies by possibly going off with the new woman agent, who had taken my place. She wanted me to be legal guardian. The Judge appointed me as such and I gave the usual bonds. Being so near me, I often gave her personal attention, buying her needed clothes or helping her otherwise. She was a favorite of mine at that time and I thought of her almost as my own. She was graduated at the head of her High School class and thus secured a scholarship from the state with which she entered the Normal School at Winona, Minnesota. She then became a successful teacher and at last married at Plainview, Minnesota. At this writing she has a beautiful baby girl. Sorrows seem to have come to her in her home and she looks to me especially for comfort and advice.

I have recorded these events not only for interest to my grandchildren, but that they may in after life learn some great lessons from these experiences and also know the work and struggles of "Grandpa Clarke." It has been a fascinating work and also one of greatest responsibility and care, and sometimes danger.

ORPHAN POEMS

The Reverend Mr. Clarke was writing about orphans long before he began his work with them. The *Sabbath Recorder* of July 5th, 1866 printed a poem written by the then sixteen-year-old lad from Brookfield, New York. It was titled *Prayer of a Sailor's Child.* This was perhaps just pure coincidence, but to add to the intrigue, immediately below his poem was an article entitled *News Boy's Lodging House* that outlined the work of none other than Charles Loring Brace with the news boy orphans of New York City! This was more than thirty-two years prior to the beginning of Reverend Mr. Clarke's work for the Children's Aid Society. A great coincidence perhaps, but interesting nonetheless. Herewith, Reverend Mr. Clarke's poem . . .

PRAYER OF A SAILOR'S CHILD

Poor and needy little child,
Saviour, God, I come to Thee;
For my heart is full of sorrow,
And no other hope have I.
Out upon the restless ocean,
There is one I dearly love -
Fold him in thine arms of pity,
Spread thy Guardian wings above.

When the winds are howling round him,
When the angry waves are high,
When black, heavy, midnight shadows,
On his trackless pathway lie;
Guide and guard him, blessed Saviour,

293

Bid the hurrying tempests stay,
Plant thy foot upon the waters,
Send thy smile to light his way.

When he lies, all pale and suffering,
Stretched upon his narrow bed,
With no loving face bent o'er him,
No soft hand about his head.
O, let kind and pitying angels,
Their bright forms around him bow;
Let them kiss his drooping eyelids,
Let them fan his fevered brow.

Poor and needy little child,
Still I raise my cry to Thee;
I have nestled in his bosom,
I have sported on his knee;
Dearly, dearly do I love him,
I, who on his breast have lain -
Pity now my desolation!
Bring him back to me again!

If it please thee, Heavenly Father,
I would see him come once more,
With his olden step of vigor,
With the love-lit smile he wore.
But, if I must tread Life's valley,
Orphaned, guideless, and alone,
Let me lose not, 'mid the shadows,
His dear footprints at my throne.

The poem below was pasted in one of Reverend Mr. Clarke's scrapbooks:

THE BUILDERS

He wrought it with grace and skill,
Pillar and dome and arches all
He fashioned to work his will.
And the men said who saw it's beauty,
"It shall never know decay,
Great is thy skill, Oh builder,
Thy fame shall live aye."

A teacher built a temple
With infinite love and care,
Planning each arch with patience
Laying each stone with prayer
None praised the unceasing efforts
None knew the wondrous plan
But the temple the teacher built
Was unseen by the eyes of man.

Gone is the builder's temple
Crumbled into the dust
Low lies each stately pillar
Food for the consuming rust.
But the temple the teacher built
Shall live while the ages roll
For the beautiful unseen temple
Was a child's immortal soul.

Author unknown.

A LETTER FROM REVEREND CLARKE
TO HIS MANY ORPHAN WARDS

Sanitarium H. P. O.
Battle Creek, Michigan

Dear Fellow Travelers,

Whether old or young, I think of friends as travelers with me to a far distant land, where, if we all meet there by and by, we will lay down pens and typewriters and have a good time talking, in no hurry to get the train or fly away to other work. We will not say, "I was so busy I could not write as soon as I intended."

But, maybe it is not so far away as we imagine, for a hundred years is not far away. Much less ten, twenty, more or less years. This just to remind you and myself that we are all "fellow travelers" no matter what our age. Let's have a good time while on the journey. But what is a "good time"? You have heard or read of the young man who needed rest and was tired of waiting on other folks and wanted to go away on a vacation all by himself for two weeks and have a good time. "Did you have a good time?," he was asked when he returned. And he said, "No." Just thinking of himself and enjoying himself, looking after his own happiness, was a miserable way to have a good time. So what an awful old world this would be if all had no interest in others.

Say, how I do wish I knew how to now write the most interesting and helpful letter of my life. But here it is again, I have a lot just now to do. I am, besides my laboratory work, averaging at least ten pages every day of writing on sheets the size of this. And yet how lonesome I'd be if none of you wrote to me. Your letters are like food and drink to me. I feast on them. And I like them if they tell about the kitchen cat and barn fowl and horses before the sleigh or wagon. I like them if they tell of your next plans or your recent pleasures. I like them when they say you are awful busy, but do not forget me. I like them if you look back over the road you have traveled and tell me what memory recalls as your most enjoyable good time. I am wondering now what it would be. But I'll make a venture to say that the best time you had was when you were saying something and doing something that put joy into the life of another. I have had two letters recently from a crippled girl in the Christian Home at Council Bluffs, Iowa, where she has been for years, only able to be in a wheel chair and who never goes to church or a movie or off visiting, and one day is like another all the time. I have had the sweetest times in writing her and sending her cards and other things. She is no relative of mine. I met her twice or three times there in my travels and somehow got to corresponding with her. I expect to continue it as long as she or I live.

I am spinning out a meditation and not saying much. You well know that I am always so glad when I hear from you. It keeps up the pleasure as we travel along on "Friendship Road." Did you ever reach a turn on that road and did not know which path to take? Be careful, but maybe there is a guide board.

Now, possibly I'll write a little more when I get to my own typewriter, which is the Underwood.

Until then, Good day,
H. D. Clarke

THE CHILDREN'S COUNTRY HOMES SOCIETY
OF CINCINNATI, OHIO

William Cooper Proctor, President
W. K. Schoeph, Vice President
John Burchenal, Treasurer
Otto Armleder, Harry McLevy, H. T. Emerson, Secretaries
H. D. Clarke, Traveling and Placing Agent

In the Spring of 1911, I received a letter from John Burchenal, General Manager of the Procter & Gamble Company of Cincinnati, Ohio, asking if I would entertain a proposition to come to Cincinnati to help build up a new Children's Home for placing homeless children as I had been or was doing for the New York Children's Aid Society. He had it seems written to Mr. R. N. Brace of the New York Society and I had been recommended as a suitable person to do this, etc. Mr. Proctor was at the head of the Ivory and Lenox Soap industry, with unlimited means for the work. Mr. Proctor's father had been deeply interested in such work and for years had been a Trustee in the Children's Home of Cincinnati. Entering in to this plan were several men of great wealth.

I wrote to Mr. Brace for his advice in the matter, though I hardly wanted to sever my long connections with the Aid Society. It may have been a mistake that I did. Mr. Brace advised my accepting the position, saying it would be an enlargement of the work and a promotion for me. I therefore went to Cincinnati to consult with Mr. Proctor and his general manager Burchenal. I was offered a salary of twelve hundred dollars a year and expenses. Returning home to consider it, I accepted the position and work, but continued to make the visits and placings of the New York Aid Society as formerly, until it was time to go to Cincinnati.

In August of 1911 I went to Cincinnati to begin preparations. There was little to do for a long time except to have an office in the General Manager's office while working out plans. The work must start from the very beginning. Mr. Proctor was to buy a large farm, which he did, three miles from Glendale, Ohio and a few miles north of Cincinnati.

I missed so much the visits with my New York wards and also being in Cincinnati, it was a long time to wait to see my dear wife. I could not as formerly, go home every two or three weeks, and until permanently and more securely settled, she could not come to stay with me. Her health was so very poor. It was a great cross to her, this separation, though she had our daughter Florence five miles away and our daughter Mabel in town until our son Charles might change his pastorate. That fall I went back home for a long visit, there being a very slow start getting ready for real work.

The new Society was incorporated in Ohio as the Children's Country Homes Society. Officers are listed above. I set out to write up a great deal of matter that would be needed when ready for business and put it in print. I helped in any way possible, with my thirteen years experience. Looking back now, I almost regret the new arrangement, for the New York Children's Aid Society workers had a life job as a rule. There were more days off and more time at home. The salary of course was about four hundred dollars less than I got in Cincinnati, but expenses at Cincinnati would be much greater.

Mr. Proctor presented the farm of ninety acres, with large buildings on it that had been enlarged. Mr. Proctor and Mr. Burchenal lived at Glendale, about four miles from the Home. A trolley line went from Glendale to Cincinnati. There was a beautiful creek near the Home and the scenery was beautiful. Here the children would be free to roam about and to play and swim and do a few farm chores when old enough. The plan was at first to take in only normal boys for placing when homes were found for them. Later on some girls were also taken in when a place was fully completed for their care. Babies of either sex could be kept. We were to get the children from the usual sources, being surrendered by guardians, juvenile authorities and municipal authorities, etc. There was an Episcopal Orphanage at

Glendale called the Bethany Home for Children. Here occasionally could be obtained children if they were not what the Home wanted to keep there to be brought up Episcopalians, which seemed to be a great, if not the greatest motive for retaining what children they had, probably from Episcopalian families. They were daily trained in the ritual of that church. I took a few from there under various circumstances.

I secured for Farm Manager and Matron, Mr. and Mrs. Frank E. Tappan of Dodge Center, Minnesota. We were to do no unnecessary farm or other work, being ourselves Seventh Day Baptists. Mr. Tappan's salary was one thousand dollars and all expenses. Everything furnished except clothing for ourselves. We hired help both for the house and the farm. Our mail came RFD. During the long summer months we had rooms in the city until the farm home was all ready. We took our meals at restaurants. The Tappans came in February of 1912 and brought my wife with them. My wife was doing very poorly and should not have come at all. Soon we were established at the Farm Home. In March I started out on a campaign to arrange Committees in many towns, mostly among the W. C. T. U's, to take or solicit applications. I gave lectures here and there on the subject and work of the society. I also made a trip to Battle Creek, Michigan, giving a lecture in the Sanitarium Chapel to our church there. This visit bore fruit in a later call to work at the Haskell Home. Pastor D. B. Coon was pastor of the Battle Creek church.

Returning to Cincinnati, I found my wife growing very weak and seriously ill. We at once returned to our home at Dodge Center, Minnesota, where she died in May of 1912. I went to Albion, Wisconsin for a few days rest on May 18th and then returned to Cincinnati the 21st to start my work again, but with my heart broken and less ambition.

Now, there was to be a very radical change in the plans and operations of the Home. The Children's Home of Cincinnati was contemplating a Farm Home and made offers to Mr. Proctor to transfer the Country Homes Society to them. This Mr. Proctor did and so we were now under different management henceforth. This was a keen disappointment to me, as well as the Tappans. The Children's

Home had another Agent who had for years been placing children and he was very jealous of my being introduced into their work, though this was under the conditions imposed by the former Society. I was to be retained by the old city Home. I was sold to the Children's Home Society of Cincinnati, with a new Superintendent and the dictation of the old agent, somewhat. This made friction. The Assistant Superintendent was a Quaker and bitterly opposed to my coming and was actually insulting. The Superintendent, Crouse, stood by me. He was a Presbyterian.

On the order of the Superintendent, I placed a girl at Norwalk, Ohio. While the Superintendent was ill and up at the Battle Creek Sanitarium a few weeks, the assistant and other agent were going to have the girl taken away at once, so he could place her where he chose. I wrote to the family who took Edna and told them to keep her and never give her up to the other man to replace. I told them I'd stand by them through thick and thin. The Superintendent stood by me in this and that made for more jealousy and friction.

On June 7th, 1912 there was a pretty sight of fifteen hundred orphan children being paraded around the city in autos that were furnished. There was a picnic dinner at Chester Park.

I began to place children in Illinois, Indiana, Ohio, West Virginia, Pennsylvania and once in Alabama. In the Autumn of 1912, at the request of Mr. Burchenal (though the Superintendent opposed it), it was decided that I make a canvass of the County Commissioners of every county in the state to induce them to give us their children that were suitable to place in homes. This would make a great saving to the counties and guarantee better protection to each child. Terms were made and I started out interviewing Commission Boards in many counties. Each county in Ohio has a home of its own. This was an experimental trip and venture. I was received with much courtesy and with encouragement by the County Commissioners, but the County Superintendents were greatly opposed to giving up their children, being anxious to make a big showing of children, as it might lessen the work and position of the County Superintendents. The reason they did not approve, of course. All in all, this proposition was a failure. Our Superintendent was positive it would not succeed, but our Trustees thought it would. The Superintendent was right, but it made me a busy man for some time.

The placing of children here was vastly different from the New York Children's Aid Society. With them I took from twelve to thirty children at a time to a town previously advertised in. I placed only one at a time for this home, as a rule only after a home had been secured and an applicant had sent in the application. The application was always investigated and approved or disapproved.

The experiences were quite different. The City Home was on Plum Street and about two hundred children at a time were there until the new County Homes were built and the Goenwood Home and farm abandoned. The children were given many excursions and picnics and many business men took many pains to give these for the children's benefit. Among those who I placed in homes we might mention just a few as samples from this Cincinnati work below:

VIOLA ASHDOWN - Three months old. Her father was a grocer clerk. Her mother deserted before the child was born. Beatrice Ashdown found the baby and brought her to the Home. On July 1st I took her to Tedrow, Ohio, placing her with a young couple in town. She was adopted and the foster mother did not want the child to ever know that she was not their own. When the child was eleven years old she wrote to me, but not knowing I was the one that placed her there. She sent me her photo. The adoptive parents are very shy about my writing to her. They do not write, but a neighbor woman of the W.C.T.U., through whom I obtained the application, writes to me.

DAVIS CHILDREN - When I was stationed at Cincinnati as placing agent, I had secured homes for wards at Salem, West Virginia. My attention was called in some way to four children of W. J. Davis, near Greenbriar, West Virginia. Greenbriar was six miles south of Salem. An elder brother of the children, Fornia, had gone to live with his uncle, Reverend R. G. Davis of Syracuse, New York. The mother died November 19th, 1911 at age thirty-seven. The father felt that he must give up his children. The children were: Jettie Andra Davis, born January 8th, 1900; dark hair, blue eyes, weighed sixty-two pounds,

Luttie Agatha Davis, born March 5th, 1902; light brown hair, blue eyes, weighed fifty-eight pounds, Ressa Arneth Davis, born April 27th, 1904; light hair, dark blue eyes, weighed forty-eight pounds, Oma May Davis, born July 14th, 1907; light hair, blue eyes, weighed twenty-five pounds.

On January 14th, 1913 I went after Oma and placed her with Professor A. B. and Hattie West at Milton, Wisconsin. My daughter Mabel met me in Chicago and took her the rest of the way. They adopted her and gave her name as Virginia West.

On February 25th, 1913 I took Luttie, Ressa and Jettie to Milton and Milton Junction, Wisconsin. Luttie and Ressa were taken by Frank and Mrs. Wells on a farm in Milton. Their names were changed to Janet, Lura and Rolla. Janet received an education in the public school, grew up a very pretty and stable young woman. She was loved and petted by foster parents and her foster sister. On Thursday, June 22nd, 1922 Janet was married to Chester Davis Newman from Jackson Center, Ohio. He graduated at Milton College in June 1922 and engaged as a teacher the following fall.

Lura stayed at Mr. Wells' until about 1919, when she came to me at Battle Creek and I sent her to her uncle, Reverend R. G. Davis in New York state. The next year she went to her father at Salem and then later to Spencer, West Virginia.

Rolla left Mr. Wells for West Virginia, but became homesick and returned. She went with the family on a long outing by auto to California in 1921 and 1922 and returned. Virginia is still with Professor West and doing finely.

DEARTH   SISTERS - Evelyn, Clara, and Mabel. These I took to different homes far apart. There was another sister named Pearl. I took them from the House of Refuge. The parents were of doubtful character. They separated. I took Clara to Bloomington, Illinois. She was a likable girl of eleven years. She had a very pleasant and respectable home. She wanted to stay, but in a year the immoral mother got in some way an order from the Court compelling the girl to be returned to her. Mabel was adopted.

GRACE AND ISAAC EDDY - There was another sister, Ruth, who had already been placed and a sister, Mary Elizabeth, still at the Bethany Home, who wanted me to take her also, but the Home refused. These two children were given to me to place by the Bethany Home (Episcopalian) because the mother was trying to get at them and coax or compel them to come with her. She had formerly showed no interest in her children and was unfit to have them. The father was dead.

I took Isaac to Janelew, West Virginia to the Davis family. He was a very nice quiet boy. There he stayed until June 1st, when he ran away, saying he was going to enlist in the Navy. He was never heard from again.

DOROTHY VIOLET HARNISH - I was in the office when the older agent and the Assistant Superintendent teased the child away from the mother. The child was about sixteen months old and one of the brightest babies I ever saw. The mother was a pretty woman and out of work and wanted the Home to care for her baby as it did for others, while the mother was getting work and able to give the child a home. But, they labored with her to show her how much better the child would be if given to them and placed in a nice home. At last she gave in and signed the papers, giving the child to the Home. It made me so indignant, but I was helpless in the matter. When she had surrendered her baby, I took her into my arms and started to take her up to the Farm Home. The mother stood in the door and the baby, waving its hand at the mother, rendered the poor mother heartbroken. She was never to see her little darling again. In a week or two I received a letter from the mother pleading for her baby to be given back to her. It was too late. The child had been taken off and already placed. I never heard from the mother again. Years passed by and I wrote to her and visited her once. She was adopted by a very talented woman who was principal of some of the city schools in Springfield, Ohio.

The girl for years never knew that she was adopted and I was not to tell the mother or others. The girl's father had paid for the board of the baby up to October of 1911. He then left the city. The mother had been working for over a year at a private home for three dollars a week, to help board the child. I have a photo of the child when a baby and several sent to me in 1927 and 1928. I do not know if she had yet been told who she is or about the mother. The girl is now, at this writing, seventeen and a half years of age. She is President of the City Club of Girls in Music. Of course, the girl is being educated and in a better home than the mother could give, but what about a brokenhearted mother, who will always mourn the loss of her baby? Is it right?

SAMUEL HAYES - Samuel was a colored boy. He was eleven years of age. I took him from the House of Refuge. His father was still living and worked in a cotton factory. The mother was dead. He had four brothers and four sisters. I took him to a colored family at St. Henry named Okay. The man was a minister in the AME church. He was not at home. The wife and son were and we arrived at dinner time. She and the boy looked Samuel over as you would a pig you were about to buy.

Soon the woman said, "I don't want him."

"Why?," I asked.

"He's too black and his hair is too curly," she replied.

"But I described him to you and you wrote and told me to bring him," I said.

"But I don't want him," she insisted.

I said, "I might have brought you an Indian with straight hair."

"I'd have taken him," she said.

I replied, "You'd better go south where white folks are not as prejudiced as you are."

We were not invited to dinner and so I drove five miles to the nearest hotel, bought the boy a good dinner and then took him back to Cincinnati.

LONNIE MORELAND - He was ten years old and a great favorite at the Farm Home. He always seemed to be so honest, but somehow he had the faculty of finding lots of pennies about the place and no one claimed to have lost any. Lonnie had been very sick with tuberculosis, but was pronounced well at the hospital. I took him to Paulding, Ohio and placed him on a farm. As the years passed there, he developed in to a first class thief and was taken to a reform school. Said a large Convention of Dutch Physicians, "No child inherits any immoral qualities." Problem. Where and how did that propensity develop so early in life?

FRED AND FRANCES STORER - These were twins and very handsome children. The whereabouts of the parents was unknown. These children were put in the House of Refuge, where I sometimes got children. The father was a carpenter. There were two older brothers. The girl had been unusually petted in the Home and seemingly spoiled for an adopted home. I placed both in the same home. Frances was exceedingly selfish and quarreled with her brother so much that the foster parents turned her off. She had dark brown hair and hazel brown eyes. She was beautiful. I replaced her. Fred later on became reckless after baptism and church relations and ran away. I had sent the boy's picture to his sister, and her foster mother refused to receive it.

THELMA TAYLOR - Thelma was a colored girl. She was seven years of age. I took her from the City Refuge. A well-to-do colored farmer took her at Celina, Ohio. Other members of the family, jealous, abused the child. She had to be removed the next year.

A sketch of all these, good and bad, would be too numerous for recording. Since I resigned and came away, officers have taken on the work of the Children's Home. Many new buildings have been built and the work enlarged. When I left Cincinnati, the *Home Record* gave me a beautiful and affectionate write up. This I appreciated, but I apprehend my leaving as a source of great pleasure to the other agent and Assistant Superintendent.

(next page). A picnic day in 1912 at the Children's Home near Cincinnati. H. D. Clarke is standing in road on the left, holding Dorothy Harnish.

One of our Picnic days
1912

Indicates H D Clarke and
tle Dorothy Harnish, now
othy Fry, of Springfield Ohio
rothy was about 15 month old

A Good Harvest

The Way We Accepted Commodore Brooks' Call

(top). Children from the Home going on a hay ride.

(bottom). Children and attendants from the home going for a boat ride on the steam boat "Princess."

Picture taken at the Annual Outing Given by Mrs. Laura Strauss

Twelve Nestlings At Our Country Home

(above). Children nestled in the hay at the Children's Home.

(right). Children from the Home "taking it all in" while overlooking the "Queen City."

(previous page). Children from the Home enjoying an ice cream cone treat.

(top). Willie Allen.

(bottom). Viola Ashdown and foster parents.

Left to right: Ressa, Lutie, Oma and Jettie Davis.

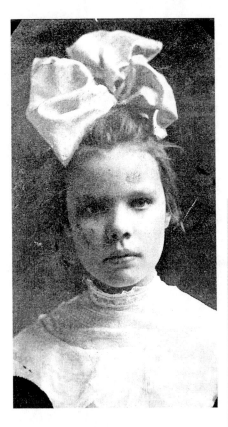

(top). Clara Dearth.

(bottom). Mabel Dearth.

(top). Evelyn Dearth.

(bottom). H. D. Clarke holding Grace
Eddy.

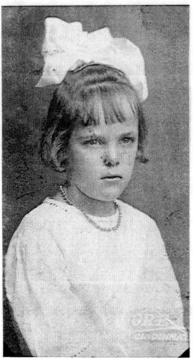

(top). Frank Ford.

(bottom). Pearl Ford.

(top). Estella Gratigne.

(bottom). Helen Gratigne.

Edna Grigsby.

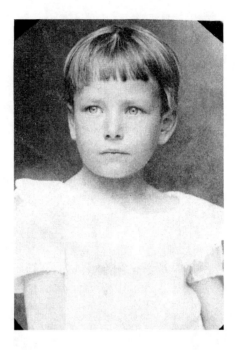

Matilda Grigsby.

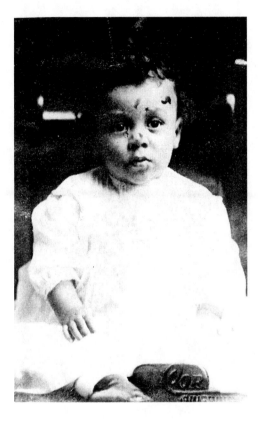

Daniel Hatfield.

Samuel Hayes.

Alice Hines.

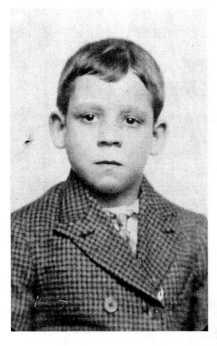

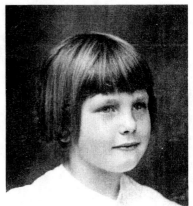

(top). John Hines.

(bottom). Freda Jones.

Harry Lowe.

Howard Lowe.

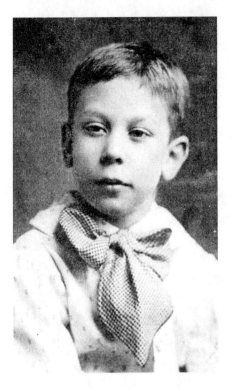

John M. Manning.

Dorothy E. McIntyre.

(top). Lonnie Moreland.

(bottom). Estella Nagel.

H. D. Clarke and Myrtle Schwab.

(top). Edna Senger in center.

(bottom). Andrew Senger.

(top). Willie Simpson.

(bottom). Lucia Smith.

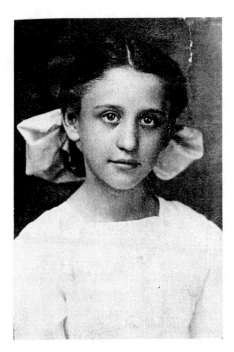

(top). Frances Storer.

(bottom). Frederick Storer.

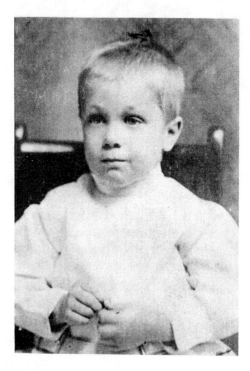

Albert Summers.

Thelma Taylor.

"THE BIRTHDAY SONG"
BY REVEREND CLARKE

Ever since I was in orphan work, I tried to keep track of their birthdays and send them a card or special letter to remind them of my kindest interest in them.

While on a visit to Albion, Wisconsin in 1915 to my son Charles and his wife Mabel's, I learned that Charles had a printing outfit. I set the type and printed the little birthday greeting seen below.

This birthday song elicited many cheering replies. It seemed to please the young people immensely. Elderly people, as a rule, do not realize the pleasure given to a child or youth by a letter. I often illustrate my letters with crayon drawings and little original jingles.

Sometimes, when I'd get flooded with letters and couldn't "catch up," I would strike off a circular letter in type like this and such as would be suitable for any or all of them, and mail it, and few would know the difference. I usually wrote about the same thing in all letters at the time of writing.

YOUR BIRTHDAY SONG

"Your life's a song; God writes the words,
And you set them to music at pleasure;
And the song grows glad, or sweet, or sad,
As you choose to fashion the measure.
You must write the music, whatever the song,
Whatever its rhyme or metre;
And if it is sad, you can make it glad,
Or, if sweet, you can make it sweeter.

THIS IS MY 1915 MESSAGE TO YOU
Kind messages, that pass from land to land
Kind letters, that betray the heart's deep history,
In which we feel the pressure of the hand, -
One touch of fire, - and all the rest is mystery!

——————————————

May you have many happy birthdays,
As ever, yours,
H. D. Clarke

THE HASKELL HOME OF
BATTLE CREEK, MICHIGAN

It was a disappointment to me to give up these visits to the dear boys and girls I had placed in homes. There was solid comfort in that work. Battle Creek seems the next place for operations. After I went there I sent for Mr. and Mrs. Tappan, then Elvan and family. This drew others to Sanitarium work until in 1924 or thereabouts, at a Dodge Centerite reunion at Coguac Lake, there were sixty or more persons who came from Dodge Center, Minnesota with their children.

To go to Battle Creek at that time was a financial sacrifice of about four hundred fifty dollars a year. This was less salary than I was getting, but I had never set a price on my labors anywhere I ever labored or whatever I did. I have always taken what was offered, and have been dealt with as well as the average.

Dr. Kellogg, at the head of the Board of Trustees of the Haskell Home, was looking for a new Superintendent. His cousin had been there for six years. The larger building had burned down. Pastor D.B. Coon of the Seventh Day Baptist Church of Battle Creek, seems to have recommended me to Dr. Kellogg. The doctor wrote to me to come up and talk matters over, which I did and finally accepted the offer given me.

The Haskell Home was established by a Mrs. Haskell of Chicago in memory of her husband, who had been (or she was) a patient at the Sanitarium. After the Home had sold off about fifteen acres of its' land, there were fifty-five acres left when I went there. There were orchards of peaches, cherries, apples and vineyards of grapes and berries. The buildings and land had greatly depredated in value from insufficient help employed and lack of care. It was a very dirty place. One room was full of antiquated clothing, such as hats, shoes, etc. that I soon burned to be rid of vermin and infection.

A committee of visitation and help of five women was organized and they furnished the Home with new furniture and clothed up the children nicely. They seemed to stand by me nobly. The largest weekly expenditure was the laundry bills, but my financial statements were always O.K.'d. I had no Matron to begin with, nor for three months after I arrived. I had a Miss Armstrong, who had been brought up in the Home as Assistant Matron in the meantime. I hired other help for inside, as well as outside work. The older girls were also made to assist. Mrs. Dr. Kellogg said I did pioneer work. Mrs. Kellogg had been an Alfred, New York girl and lived opposite the Greenes where I roomed when at Alfred while going to school. Miss Armstrong had two brothers and a sister in the Home. The brothers were now hired men. Helen, the younger sister was much help. In later years I found Helen a place to stay and attend High School at Dodge Center, Minnesota. I worked from 5:00 a.m. to 10:00 p.m. constantly and saw but very little of the city.

I made out a weekly menu for the tables and knew what every meal was to be every day for a week ahead. The kitchen help followed my directions. Mrs. Kellogg helped me arrange the menu. My own private room was at the head of the stairs on the second floor, where I could oversee both girls and boys dormitories or floors. The boys were on the third floor. The children retired at eight p.m. and were up at six a.m. We had devotions each morning before breakfast. On Sabbath days we had special talks, illustrated by crayons on the black board. On Sabbath morning we walked by twos to the Sanitarium Chapel for a Union Sabbath School. I did not compel the wards to attend preaching services in the afternoon, but any who wished, went with me.

There were three pianos in the Home and a mechanical musical machine. The former Superintendent had strictly forbidden the children to enter the office on the first floor, but I humored them. It gave them pleasure to step in and be with me. We had a good library there. The dining room was large with three large tables and a small one. I had my special table to which the hired help was admitted. I soon had my Helen Gratigne, who is mentioned among my special guardian group elsewhere.

At mealtime the children marched in from the play and reception room and were not permitted to talk, as soon it would be bedlam if all were buzzing away. I never whipped but one boy in the Home and he was the very best boy of all. The soul of honor, but he once had a very stubborn streak and would not obey. My punishments were usually sending them to stay in their room for a given period, according to the offense committed.

One girl had quite a talent for composing a theatrical play, in which I indulged her and then had quite an entertainment. The Home admitted boys and girls for boarding by their parents or guardians at two dollars a week. After three months of very strenuous work I secured a Matron in Miss Flora Burdick, of Alfred, New York. At this time also came Mamie Gunderson, whom I have mentioned on another page. I paid her more than she asked for her splendid work and devotion to it. I then made her Assistant Matron. Miss Burdick was lovely and of a good disposition and was patient, although she would assume no special control of the wards as far as government was concerned or when any special need of it came. Late in the season her stepmother was sick and soon died and Miss Burdick left me. I was again for a time without a Matron. Later on I secured Mrs. Flora Tappan, who came with her family from the Children's Home Farm near Cincinnati, Ohio. They had resigned their work there.

Of the children who we had and those who boarded with us, much could be said of interest. On holidays we had great times. Picnics, amusement at the Lake, Chatauquas. I bought a hundred feet of water hose and while sprinkling the lawns they had a great time with that. There was great fun for a boy or girl holding the hose. I gave all who would till a square rod or two of ground for a garden, offering a prize for the best, but they had little interest. The fifteen acres of land that had been sold required that I build two short streets, each about two blocks long. For this I engaged men and made the ex-Superintendent boss of the gang. The bill for this street grading was about fifty dollars a day. The Doctor had a park of his own about five blocks away, which the Home children had the use of under the rules that governed. In picking fruit the children received the usual percent and some started bank accounts. They picked by the quart.

All children of proper age attended the public schools. We kept five horses and one cow, but the horses were ring boned and spavined and had the heaves. I gave away and sold some. I had difficulty in curing the children of a habit of throwing away or hiding their clothes or shoes when they wanted new ones. The ex-Superintendent was an Adventist minister and had baptized a few of the wards, but they did not unite with any church and soon were altogether forgetful of their baptism. A matter not altogether confined to orphan children.

In placing children in homes, each county has a commissioner whose business it is to make investigation of every one that applies for a child. He takes his time for it and is governed by his prejudices, and therefore it takes quite a while to place one child out in a home for adoption. In a few cases the ward's expense of placing was met by the Home. On one occasion I thus sent a girl named Agnes Ross to California to her stepfather. Ruth, her sister, I sent to an Adventist Elder at Osawa, Canada. There she attended a school of that church. Alice McPeek was a ladylike mulatto, who at last went back to her father. There were two sisters named Fox. A favorite among the little girls was one Helen Confer. She and my Helen Gratigne were quite chums. Willie Allen was quite attached to me and later used to write as also did his mother, in appreciation of his care. There were two Confer brothers that were some care in governing. One went to the World War. One of my helpers had three children for us to care for. The father was in jail. The mother was destitute.

This Haskell work was about the hardest and most strenuous of my life and the poorest paid. The Trustees paid little or no attention to the Home and did not visit it. One, the Secretary of the board said, "Brother Clarke, it is a one man affair. Dr. Kellogg has his hand on it as he has on the Sanitarium and when he needs we will respond, but we've had no board meeting in two years." I was told to give away as many of the children as possible and I reduced the number down to twenty-four. I was told by the doctor not to take in any more, but a homeless mother, half starved, came to me pleading for me to take their children. I could not refuse some and took them, though I do not think the doctor knew it. I think I turned away as many as fifty during the summer. It was a pitiable sight, like turning a mother and child out in to the street with nowhere to go and nothing to eat.

In the Fall of 1913, the doctor demanded that I give all the children away but a dozen and take them to the "Old Peoples Home." That Home was a Seventh Day Adventist Home for the aged and all but two had gone. That Home was soon bought by the Sanitarium. I knew that it could not be done at once, as he expected, but would take years. Again, he made the demand and in my desperation I resigned the office and left the care of the children to Mrs. Tappan. It took over five years to give the children away. I considered that act of the doctor's as almost a sin and it was very hard on me. It did not do justice to the donor of the Home funds. I surmised that the funds were turned in to the College that the doctor was intending to establish and eventually did, at Battle Creek. Following this Haskell Home resignation, I made my first real visit and vacation and went for three months on a trip east.

This was a big disappointment and made me lose four years of work before being able to secure another job. It was the end of a life's work that I could have kept on doing, had I still been with the New York Aid Society. I had worked about fifteen years at this orphan work and consider it my last and greatest work, which I had hoped to do the rest of my working days. My wife was dead, having shared with me the sacrifices and toils of it. The work brought me great happiness. It now ended, but in the years since, I have been able to do much for the ones who have been placed, and some work independent of any society or orphanage.

Photos of the Haskell Home and some of the children appear on the pages that follow:

Children and attendants marching from the Haskell Home to the Sanitarium Chapel for Union Sabbath School.

Posed with the children of Haskell Home are H. D. Clarke (far right) and Mamie
Gunderson (back left).

(top). Helen and Pearl Armstrong.

(bottom). J. B. Eno (r) and Ivan Confer (l).

(top). Alex Eno.

(bottom). Ruth Ross.

CLOSING WORDS FROM REVEREND CLARKE

It is possible that I may add more to this sketch before having it bound, but lest I should not, I wish to add here that this first writing of it has taken nearly three years, writing from time to time. It is very incomplete, though voluminous. My fifteen years service would make a much larger book than I could write. There are many, many experiences and incidents that I feel sure in years to come will be of interest to the grandchildren, for whom I have written this, and am greatly attached. Possibly, in some other books or stories, they will have added information they will love to preserve in memory of their grandfather Clarke. If I never live to prepare a volume for each grandchild, it is my hope that some of my children will see that copies are made for each. In the years to come, in the providence of God, it may be that these chapters will be of much interest and the historical parts of use to some future historian. That it may especially help my grandchildren to do better than I have done, and to encourage them to "strive for the mastery" is my earnest prayer.

Many orphan girls and boys have grown up and since I commenced this sketch have married, and some have died. Some of these children have become school teachers, book keepers, stenographers, clerks, electricians, lawyers, ministers, judges, housewives, farmers, mechanics and many other professions. My records show that a larger percent have gone through high schools and entered colleges than is the published average among others in this nation. This is because we insisted that they should not be kept at home for plowing and other work when school was in session, a thing many farmers do to their own children, especially boys.

Letters keep coming in great numbers. Occasionally, one wants his or her history, or to be told where their people are and whether they have any brothers or sisters or parents living. This makes my records of great value, though they are incomplete. My great files of letters have also been of value for many purposes. It has taken a vast deal of time and much expense. I trust it has been of service for good.

To my dying day I shall have deepest interest in the work of placing and caring for orphan or homeless children. Some dear friends say it was the greatest work of my life. The God of the orphan is the judge of that. The work has brought me greatest happiness and in a few cases, great grief and misunderstanding, or rather disappointment. The thousands of letters from them and their homes all these years testify to the success of it, and to their appreciation in so many cases. They will remember him, who turned the tides of their lives for the better, and for eternity.

If God in His mercy shall give me a place in heaven, I hope to see among the redeemed, many of these souls who were snatched from poverty and woe and given a home with advantages on earth, and grew up respectable citizens.

Grace and peace to my grandchildren,

Herman D. Clarke

May 2nd, 1917
15 Read Terrace
Battle Creek, Michigan

WHERE TO WRITE FOR INFORMATION ABOUT ORPHAN TRAIN RIDERS

Brooklyn Nursery and Infants Hospital:
c/o Salvation Army
Foster Home and Adoption Services
233 East 17th Street
New York, NY 10003

Children's Aid Society:
Office of Closed Records
Attention: Victor Remer
150 East 45th Street
New York, NY 10017
PH: 212-949-4800

Children's Village records (Formerly New York Juvenile Asylum):
Children's Village
c/o Office of Alumni Affairs
Dobbs Ferry, NY 10522

Five Points House of Industry, Greer-Woodycrest and Hope Farm
Records:
Mr. Mark Lukens, Director
Crystal Run Village
RD 2, Box 98
Middletown, NY 10940

Home for Destitute Children (formerly the Brooklyn Industrial School,
Established 1854) and later the Brooklyn Home for Children Records:
c/o Forestdale, Inc.
67-35 112th Street

Forest Hills, NY 11375-2349
PH: 718-263-0740
Open Monday through Friday (9-5 p.m.)

New York Child's Foster Home Services, Sheltering Arms and Speedwell Records:
c/o Sheltering Arms
122 East 29th Street
New York, NY 10016

New York Infant Asylum Records (merged in 1910 with New York Nursery and Child's Hospital):
c/o Mrs. Adele Lerner
Medical Archives
NY Hospital Cornell Medical Center
1300 York Ave.
New York, NY 10021

Orphan Train Heritage Society of America (OTHSA)
614 East Emma Avenue, Suite 115
Springdale, AR 72764-4634
PH: 501-756-2780
FAX: 501-756-0769
E-mail: mej102339@aol.com
Website: http://pda.republic.net/othsa
(Publishes a newsletter, maintains archives and holds orphan train rider reunions across America)

St. Joseph by the Sea (Staten Island) Records:
c/o New York Foundling Hospital
Department of Closed Records
18 West 18th Street
New York, NY 10001

The Orphan Asylum Society of Brooklyn Records:
Brookwood Child Care

25 Washington
Brooklyn, NY 11201
PH: 718-596-5555
Note: They have records back to 1855. Original records are held by:
University of Minnesota-Social Welfare History Archives
101 Walter Library
117 Pleasant Street, S.E.
Minneapolis, MN 55455
PH: 612-624-4377
FAX: 612-625-5525
Note: They will search the records for you at the University or will
allow others to do so.

The Orphan Asylum Society (City of New York) Records:
c/o Graham-Windham Services to Families and Children
One South Broadway
Hastings-on-Hudson, NY 10706
PH: 212-529-6445
PH: 914-478-1100 (Westchester Branch)

FOR FURTHER READING

Nonfiction

Brace, Charles Loring. *The Dangerous Classes of New York and Twenty Years' Work among Them*. New York: 1880. Reprint, New Jersey: Patterson Smith, 1967.

Children's Aid Society. Annual Reports 1-10. New York: 1854-1863. Reprint, Arno Press and New York Times, 1971 (now handled by Ayer Company Publishers, Salem, New Hampshire).

Fry, Annette Riley. *"The Children's Migration." American Heritage*, December 1974, 4-10.

Holt, Marilyn Irvin. *The Orphan Trains: Placing Out in America*. Lincoln, Nebraska: University of Nebraska Press, 1992.

Jackson, Donald Dale. *"It Took Trains to Put Street Kids on the Right Track Out of the Slums." Smithsonian*, August 1986, 95-103.

Johnson, Mary Ellen, and Kay B. Hall. *Orphan Train Riders, Their Own Stories*. Vols. 1-5. Baltimore: Gateway Press, 1992, 1993,

Wheeler, Leslie. *"The Orphan Trains," American History Illustrated*, December 1983, 10-23.

Fiction

De Vries, David. *Home at Last*. New York: Dell, 1990.

Holland, Isabelle. *The Journey Home*. New York: Scholastic, 1990.

Nixon, Joan. *The Orphan Train Quartet: A Family Apart, Caught in the Act, In the Face of Danger, A Place to Belong*. New York: Bantam Books, 1988-1990.

Peart, Jane. *Orphan Train West Trilogy: Homeward the Seeking Heart, Quest for Lasting Love, Dreams of a Longing Heart*. Tarrytown, New York: Fleming H. Revell Co., 1990.

Petrie, Dorothea G., and James Magnuson. *Orphan Train*. New York: Dial Press, 1978.

Talbot, Charles Joy. *An Orphan for Nebraska*. New York: Atheneum, 1979.

ADDENDA

The following article was written by Rev. Clarke about Una Church for *The Sabbath Visitor*. Una came out with the Chatfield, Minnesota company of January 8th, 1903. See page 69.

"Una Church. Is not that a pretty name for a pretty girl? Yes, but a strange thing about it is, that while she is, as near as we can guess, seven years old, she has had a name only since Jan. 5, 1903. And that date, too, is hereafter to be her birthday for presents, or parties, or anything connected with birthdays.

Seven years old Jan. 5th and never had a real name, or a birthday till then! How can that be? Well, some of the readers of THE SABBATH VISITOR already know about it for we told the story in a Sabbath-school recently, but the rest of you will be interested in it.

A little girl, seemingly about three years old was picked up in the streets of the great city of New York and taken to a Home for destitute children. She was so weak and so destitute that she could not speak a word in many, many days. No father or mother was ever found; no friend ever claimed her. She was fed and clothed at the Home for four years until she was a healthy, rosy-cheeked, beautiful girl, bright, intelligent, active.

In December, the writer of this story went to a town in Minnesota to arrange for the placing of orphan boys and girls in good homes as he has done in other towns. Jan. 8, 1903 was the day set for the company, in charge of a good man and a nurse, to meet us at that place. There were nine good orphan boys and five sweet little girls. Among them was Una. Before she started with the rest of the company, the Unitarian Church, of Yonkers, N. Y. sent, as is its custom, a nice little sum of money to the Society to pay the fare of some poor child needing a home. As the one to receive this help from that church, this little girl was selected. She had no real name and no birthday. So the

Yonkers Unitarian Sunday-school named January 5th for her birthday and called her, Una Church, and now she is in a happy home, with a foster papa and mamma to love her and teach her how to develop into a good and useful woman.

When we first took her little hand, she gave us a kiss of friendship, and now we must visit her every year and see that she is properly cared for and loved in the new home. She is happy and contented.

Will all the boys and girls who read the VISITOR be as happy in the love and care of God, with their own parents and in their own dear homes as they ought to be? If you are ever discontented and do not have all you want, stop and think of the thousands who have no homes, no fathers and mothers; think of Una Church and how God loved and cared for her when forsaken by those who ought to have given her love and a home."

INDEX

CRONKHITE, George 121 Mrs George
121
CULVER, S H 86
CUMMINGS, Franklin 196
CUNNA, Herman 121
D, Frances 139
DAILEY, Annie Jane 148 150 Dorothy
148 150 157 James 148 Thomas 174
DALARA, David 200-201 205 Fannie
201 Fanny 200-201 205
DANIELS, Ida 115 180 J H 115 180
DASHIELL, Elizabeth 285 Mark 285
Mark Jr 287 Mrs Mark 286
DAUMAN, Margaret 69-70
DAVENPORT, Amos 151 Lawrence
151 Luella Maude 148 151 158
Maudie 151
DAVIE, Anna 132 135 Annie 142 W A
121
DAVIS, 305 Cecil 209-210 262 Fornia
303 Janet 304 Jettie 314 Jettie
Andra 303 John 215-217 Lura 304
Lutie 314 Luttie Agatha 304 Oma
314 Oma May 304 R G 303-304
Ressa 314 Ressa Arneth 304 Rolla
304 W J 303
DEACON, Charles 86
DEARTH, Clara 282 304 315 Evelyn
304 316 Mabel 304 315 Pearl 304
DECKER, Boy 186 James 179-180
Jennie 179-180 186 William 179-
180
DEL VECCHIO, Angelina 272-273
Anna 272 Domico 272 Marie 272-
273 Philomena 272-273 Philomena
Phila 273
DEMOURJIN, Thomas 40 43
DENAIRO, Carmine 29-30 34 Jesse 34
Jessie 29-30
DENHAM, J B 221
DENISON, Mr 225
DENNIS, Don 138 Frances 138 140
DENNY, Cecil 106 109 Eddy 106
DENSMOORE, Mrs Fred 215

DEROCHER, Cora 200-201 205
DESIMPLE, Julian 289
DEVOS, 201
DEVOSS, Jacob 44
DICKENSON, Jennie 167 171 Mabel
240 Maggie 167 171 Nellie 167-168
171
DICTING, Harry 113 116 William 113
Willie 116
DIVINE, Patrick 44 69-70
DOANE, W E 242
DOER, John 209-210
DORAN, Eliza 69-70 76 Lizzie 79-80
DOYLE, Alfred 232 Ethel 233 Howard
232 Isadore 237 Isadore Ethel 232
James 232-233 237 William 240
DRENNAN, D D 79
DUGAN, Mary 28
DUKE, W L 86
DUMLER, Charlotte 233 Emanuel 233
DUNCAN, Ethel May 186-187 189
DUTTON, William S 27
EAGEN, Elizabeth 113-114 116 118
James 114
EARL, I T 94 Lillian 94
EASLEY, James 174-175 Ms 175
EDDY, Grace 305 316 Isaac 305 Mary
Elizabeth 305 Ruth 305
EDMOND, Mario Henry 62
EDWARDS, D A 86
EHRET, Lottie 154
ELLIS, Arthur 1 Arthur E 29 Florence
O 1 Mark 69 T S 167
EMERSON, H T 299
EMICK, Tracy 179-180 184
ENGLE, Glenn 96
ENGLER, Amelia 36 39
ENO, Alex 347 J B 346
ERICKSON, Arthur 106 Axel 255
Cecil 107 Frank 106 George 106
ERNST, W H 287
FAHR, Amanda 29 31 35 Harry 31 Ida
31 35 Ida May 29 William 31
FARMER, B F 45 Mr 46

FAUST, William 242
FENDEL, Jacob 167-168 170
FERGUSON, E M 242
FINGER, Ernest 262 Floyd 262
FINLEY, L;ouis 75 Walter 75
FLEISCHANER, Minnie 94-95 100
FLEISCHMANN, Henry 174
FLEMING, Nelson 94 96 100
FORD, Frank 317 Pearl 317
FORGY, R J 250
FORSTMAN, John 62
FORSYTHE, 288 Mr 287 Mrs 287
FORT, Geo L 45
FOWLER, 25
FOX, 342
FREDERICKS, Amelia 148 151 159
GAIDE, George 274 Pearl 274 Pearle
    274
GALETA, Samuel John 143
GARDINER, J P 167
GARDNER, J B 132 136 Ray 136
GARTLAND, Charles 148 152 160
GEE, Fred 132 135 143
GELETA, Samuel 135 Samuel John
    132
GEORGE, Daniel 79-80 83
GILLENLY, Henry 200-201
GIPSON, Mrs Solomon 121 Solomon
    121
GLASSCOCK, 154
GODFREY, Clarkson 167
GOEGEL, Alfred 240
GORDON, 179
GOUDIE, M C 167
GOULD, John 36-37
GRACE, H P 28
GRATIGNE, Estella 318 Helen 318
    340 342
GREASON, Lettie 196
GREENE, 340
GREENWOOD, Joseph 121
GRIGSBY, Edna 319 Matilda 320
GROSS, Edward 86
GROWTHER, Harold 215 217

GUNDERSON, Alfred 196 Frederick
    196 Irene 250-251 253 Mamie 196-
    198 251 341 345 Mamie May 250
    May 253 Thomas 250-251 259
HAGEN, Elizabeth 221 223 Lizzie 221
    Walter 221
HAGERTY, T M 44
HALPIN, Charles 28
HALTECOTE, Mrs 88
HANEY, Albert 225 H J 79
HANSEN, Thomas 250
HANSON, Edna 124-125 Guy 124
    Henry 250
HARBERT, John 86
HARDTKE, William 255
HARE, Cris 38 Emma 38
HARMON, Thomas 154
HARNISH, Dorothy 307 Dorothy
    Violet 305
HARRIS, Bertha 79-80 82
HARRISON, Paulina 167-168 172
HARTWOCK, Boy 179 Mabel 179-180
HASKELL, Mrs 339
HASLER, Paul 86
HASTEDT, Henry 106-107 110 Mary
    106-107 110
HATCHEN, C C 209
HATFIELD, Daniel 321
HAUGEN, S K 53
HAWKS, Helen 121 124 129
HAYDEN, Fred 225 227 Homer 200-
    201 Willie 200-201 206
HAYES, Samuel 306 322
HEGWOOD, Lizzie 174 190
HEILMAN, August 201 Augusta 36 38
    44 50 Emma 36-38 44 50 Ernest 36
    38 50 William 38
HEING, Charles 53
HEINTZ, Alexander 114 Blanch 114
    Blanche 113 116 118 George 113-
    114 116 118 Grace 114 Matilda
    113-114 116 118
HENDERSON, George 216 225 John
    215 Mr 285 Mrs 285

HENWOOD, Harry 121 124 132
HERMANCE, Allen 200 Charles 200-201 207 Frances 201 Francis 200 Frank 207 Robert 201
HERNDON, Mrs Frank 106
HEULMAN, Florence 215-217 219
HICKEY, Elizabeth 79 82 Maggie 285
HICKEY-HENDERSON, Elizabeth 285
HIGHBROWN, Edward 200-201
HILL, Alfred 226 229 Alpha 225-226 Anna L 200 225 Anna Laura 79 133 233 242 244 Miss 22 Ms 149 175 227 232 262
HINES, Alice 323 John 324
HOAGLAND, Claude 53-54 58
HOLMAN, William 113 119 Willie 115-116
HOLMES, Cora 132 William 132
HOMAN, Maurice 86
HOOK, Ruth 79-80
HOUCH, 272
HOWARD, Alma 209 Alta 123 Fred 123
HUBER, Anna 196 Freda 196
HUDSON, Edna 255 F A 86
HUGGARD, Benjamin 63 65 Benjamin Dale 62 Dale 63 George 62 Thomas 62-63 65
HUNECKE, William 28
HUNT, Margaret 174 Robert 174 Sarah 174
INGLIS, Marie Lois 290
IVEY, Doty 134
JACKET, Abram 255
JACKS, J M 38
JACKSON, J A 45 L M 167
JACOBSON, Adolphina 101 Adolphina Dorotha 94 Emma 94 102
JAMES, Ryan 190
JELLIFF, Frederick 86
JENNINGS, Anna M 1 Maria 1 Stephen 132
JEROLAMON, Arthur 86
JEWEL, Boy 94

JOHNSON, Andrus 137 Annie 53 59 Boy 167 E M 232 240 250 Harry 250-251 Ida 113 115-116 119 179-180 John 115 167-168 172 250-251 Johnnie 86 Mary 115 148 255 Willie 44 47
JONES, Carl 168 Frank 121 Freda 324 Louis 29 31 44 51 Nellie 168 Willie 121
JORDAN, A N 121 Mrs A N 121
JURISH, E A 44
KAHERBECK, August 36 38 51
KAHERBECK-BENNETT, August 44
KAHNIS, Florence 225-226 229 232 238
KAISER, H G 36
KELLERAN, Berta P A 187 Marian 186
KELLEY, G W 250
KELLOGG, Dr 339 342 Mrs 340
KELSON, 263 A R 262 Mabel 263
KEMPER, George 121
KEMPLE, C E 44
KENT, Blanch 167-168 Blanche 173 George 168 Maud 167-168 173
KERR, Urias 29 31
KIDDER, Earl 244 Emily 244
KIMBERLY, Mrs Frank 167-168
KIMMEL, Charles 113 116
KIMMERLEE, Edward 69-70
KING, Harry 44 69-70 78 S 232 Sadie 152 Walter 152
KINGSLAND, Edna 215-217 220 Harry 215-216 220 Walter 215-217 220
KITCHEN, Helen 179-180 184 Henrietta 179-180 184
KNAPP, Mr 291 Mrs 291
KOCK, Oscar 86
KOOVASTEEH, Andrew 196
KREITCHEN, Michael 86
KRUPER, John 232-233 238
KULTZ, Christopher 221
KURTH, Ben 242

LA VIGNE, Boy 79 Twins 94 Willard 79-80
LACHNAEUR, George 53
LACHNAUER, George 29
LANDBERG, Ernest 44
LANDERS, Freda 174 Lizzie 174
LANGE, Eugene 53 55 59 Fred 55
LANGWORTHY, A N 29-30 Mr 34 Mrs 34 Mrs A N 29-30
LARSON, Arthur 232-233 239 Carl 232-233 Edwin 232-233
LASSEN, Otto 44
LAUCHNEAUR, George 55
LEE, Frank 44 47
LINDBURG, Ernest 47 Gustave 69-70
LINDERGREN, Bernice 242-244 247
LINDSLEY, Clarendon 132 136 144
LINN, Bertie 222 Matilda 222 S C 222
LINVILLE, Alice 233 Don 233
LIZZIE, Doran 70
LODS, Emil 240
LOTZ, Lonnie L 135 Rosa 135
LOUCKS, C J 44
LOWE, Harold 53 55 59 Harry 325 Howard 326
LYMAN, A S 121 Mrs A S 121 Mrs John 138
MACK, Mrs 282
MACKEY, Edward 86
MAGNUS, Benjamin 196
MALONE, Elizabeth 121 Mrs Ora 121 Ora 121 Risin 121
MALONY, William 28
MANNING, John M 327
MANSFIELD, William 113 115 Willie 116
MARDY, Mary 168
MARSHALL, Mr 42
MARTIN, Ada 137 Dr 88 Jannette 89
MAY, Fred 121 Mrs Fred 121
MCCANN, Annie 152 James 152 160-161 John 152 Julia 152 Mamie 152 Martha 152 160-161 Sadie 152 160
MCCARTY, Edward 262 Marguerite

MCCARTY (cont) 262
MCCONKEY, Bessie 96 George E 96
MCCUNE, Leonard 114
MCCURDY, Mr 95
MCDONALD, Myron 250
MCGHIE, Jas 44
MCGILLIVARY, Donald 44
MCGUIRE, Florence 31 255-256 259 George 29
MCINTOSH, Elizabeth 240 Jennie 225
MCINTYRE, Dorothy E 328
MCKENZIE, Harry 167 173 275
MCKIBBEN, Edna 287-288 Elsie 287
MCLAUGHLIN, Clara 148
MCLEVY, Harry 299
MCLOY, Catherine 124
MCMANN, James 148 Martha 148 Sadie 148
MCPEEK, Alice 342 Clarence 136 George 53 George L 60 Mrs Clarence 136 Worth 55
MEDLER, Harry 175 Paul 174-175 179 Viola 175
MELROSE, Edward 121
MELVILLE, Ethel 69-70 72-73 77
METZGER, Lizzie 221
MILBURN, Grace 262-263
MILLER, A R 86 Eddie 86 Harry 69 J H 86 Mr 90 Pauline 53 55 William 132
MITCHEL, Jim 114-115 Joseph 240
MOIDEK, F J 108
MOORE, M V 87 Mr 123
MORAN, Valentine 86
MORELAND, Lonnie 306 329
MOULD, David 269 Judge 268
MOYAN, Rosa 180 183 196 268
MULLER, Christoph 179
MURPHY, Florence 276
MYERS, Herman 53
NAGEL, Estella 329
NARR, Frances 209-210 213 Grace 209-210 212 Lester 209-210 212

NEARY, George 196 Harold 196 Lillie 196
NEILBREN, Clara 190
NEIMAN, Fred 53 William 53
NELSON, Albert 123 Lena 123 Sarah 123
NEWBERT, Ernestine 79-80 83
NEWELL, Mr 36
NEWMAN, Bennie 44 48 52 Chester Davis 304 Janet 304
O'BANION, E W 121 Mrs E W 121
O'BRIAN, Patrick 28
O'CONNELL, Bertha 154 George 154
O'DAY, Valentine 148 153 161 255-256
OAKE, Harold 179
OBELL, Clarice 280-282 John Jr 280 Mr 281 Mrs 280-282
OGDEN, Eleanor 200-201
OKAY, 306
OLDS, S L 45
OLIVER, George 255
ORKIN, H B 280
ORPHAN, Albert S 265 Andrew M 275 Archie K 179 Arthur L 179 Carl 265 Cecil D 266 D D 151 Daisy 89 Daniel P 265 Edna 302 Edward 266 Emma 72 Emma C 272 Ernest 266 Floyd 266 Francis B 42 George 62 Grace W 266 Helen 9 Henry 42 Henry F 215-216 Isaac 264 John 89 Juliette 89 Lewis B 265 Lillie 28 Madeline H 186 Marguerite 266 Mary Louise 289 Minnie U 279 Mortie 28 Mortimer 28 Nathan 89 Nora H 186 Ramond 265 Sadie B 265 Wardner 28 Wilber Main 187 Wilbur Main 186
ORR, Samuel 242 244
OSTERHANDT, Lewis 86
PAINE, Daniel 262-263
PALM, Lizzie 268-269
PALMER, Annie 136 George 136 Helen 79-80 153 Marian 132 136

PALMER (cont)
   145 Marion 136 Mrs P J 44 Peter V 79
PAPE, Elsie 225-226 Harry 225-226
PARISH, E F 215
PARKER, C U 242-243 Mrs C U 242
PATRICK, Charles 148 Louise 148 152 R T 280
PEARCE, C S 168 Paulina 168 W L 168
PEARSONS, Lutie 179
PECK, Bertha 186 Edwin M 186
PERRY, Gertrude 242-244
PETERSON, Alfred 126 Lee 250-251
PHILLIPS, C B 136 Mrs C B 136
PICELLE, Samuel 116 120
PICELLE-THOMPSON, Samuel 113
PIERCE, Kittie 242 Matt 242
PLANK, Dell 132
POFF, Fred 221 Lizzie 221
PONTON, Herbert 86
POWELL, C H 190
PRITCHARD, Mr 263
PROCTOR, Mr 300-301 William Cooper 299
PULLMAN, Eva C 122
QUINCE, 191 Alice 174-176 178 190 Bella 174-176 190 Mamie 176 William 176
RANDLETTE, David 200 Fred 200
RANDOLPH, 6 Elsie 276-277 Maggie 276-277
RAPP, Frank 221 John 221-222 224 Louise 224 Lucy 232-233 Lucy Louise 221 Margaret 221
RATHBURN, D W 45
RECK, Edward 250-251 Mr 89 Wick 251
REED, Walter 44
REESE, Emily 242-244 248
REGAN, Dennis 86
REID, Eddie 86
REIDER, R J 135 Reva 135
REMER, Anthony 29

365

STALEY, Robert 121
STANTON, Jas 44 Mr 48
STAUBER, Joseph 278
STEINBECK, Henry 167
STENGER, Fred 29
STEVENS, Edna 31 Frank 31 Ina
    Lillian 29 31 62-63 66
STOLZ, Ethel 187 Roy 187
STORER, Frances 307 333 Fred 307
    Frederick 333
STOTLER, J P 148 154 Mr 79
STRENCHER, Nathan 86
STROBEL, Caroline 106-107 110
    Eddie 107
SUMMERS, Albert 334
SUNDAY, Billy 151
SUTTON, E M 45
SWAN, J W 233 Mr 232 250
SWANSON, Alice 175 C V 175
SWARTZ, W W 113
SWAYZ, Kenneth 225 227
SWAYZE, Kenneth 227
TAGGERT, E N 106
TAINTER, Mrs Clarence 282
TALLMAN, Bessie 149 Charles C 149
TAPPAN, Flora 341 Frank A 301 Mr
    339 Mrs 339 343 Mrs Frank A 301
TAYLOR, A C 148 David 87 Mrs 216
    Mrs M 44 Mrs M E 215 217 Pate 86
    Thelma 307 335
TERRY, R W 44
THAYER, E W 45
THEREIN, Howard 132 Oliver 132
THOMAS, Homer 132 137 146 Horace
    132 137 Otto 200
THOMPSON, Samuel 116 120 Samuel
    (picelle) 115 Walter 44
TICE, B W 53 79 92 148 Mr 69 149
    154 190-191 197 272
TINGLEY, Spencer 69 73
TOBISEN, Walter 86
TOMLINSON, Claude 209 214 Mary
    209-210 213 Willie 209
TOWNSEND, Floyd 225 227 231

TRAVIS, Blanche 125 C D 125
TRENDLE, George A 182 Rosa 182
TROTT, E 27 29 Mr 32 36 40
TROY, Mae 108 110 Mary 107 May
    106
TRYON, A R 132
TURK, Edna 62 67 Frank 62 Ralph 62-
    63 68
TURNER, Edna 121 124-125 129
    Grace 125 130 Henry 121 124
TURNER-GRETMAN, Grace 121
VALENTINE, Bessie 96 103 Elizabeth
    96 Flossie 96 Guy 94 Morris 94 96
    104 Raymond 94 96 104 Willis 94
VALENTINE-EARL, Bessie 94
VAN DER SHUR, M J 287
VAN DER SHURR, Beulah 287-288
VAN HORN, Lou 285 Willard 148
VAN SLYKE, Mr 121 Mrs 121
VAN WICKLEN, Daniel 174
VANSLYKE, William Jennings 29
VATH, Mrs 151
VELTA, Herbert L 256
VERMILYEA, Lillian 174 176
VETTER, Charles 29 32 94 96 105 Joe
    32 94 96
VOLKHART, Florence 121 148 153
    174 178 George 121 124 153-154
    174
WADE, Minnie 200 202
WAGGONER, 210 Margaret 209 W J
    209
WAINWRIGHT, S E 190
WALKER, B S 79
WALLACE, Amanda 121 125 131
    Charles 197 Lillian 121 125 131
    Thomas Demourjin 41
WALTER, Rosa 153 Theodore 153
WARNER, Mr 32
WARREN, W A 45
WATSON, Charles 255 257 260 J R 86
    Marie 209 Oswald G 255 R H 209
WATT, Bettie 240
WATTS, Hazel 251 254